A Basketmaker in Rural Japan

A Basketmaker

in Rural Japan

Louise Allison Cort • Nakamura Kenji

WEATHERHILL, New York and Tokyo *in association with the*
ARTHUR M. SACKLER GALLERY, Smithsonian Institution, Washington, D. C.

© 1994 by Smithsonian Institution
All rights reserved
Published by the Arthur M. Sackler
Gallery, Smithsonian Institution,
Washington, D.C., in association with
Weatherhill, Inc., New York and Tokyo
Printed in Hong Kong

Published on the occasion of an exhibition
at the Arthur M. Sackler Gallery,
November 20, 1994–July 9, 1995
Second printing, 1996

Front Cover: Hiroshima Kazuo; photograph by Louise Cort
Back cover: detail of a storage basket;
photograph by John Tsantes
Frontispiece: Hiroshima Kazuo finishes
the rim of a backpack basket; photograph
by Tabushi Satoru, courtesy of *Ginka*

Photo credits
Tazaki Tsutomu: pp. 12, 15, 19, 20, 23,
26; Tabuchi Satoru, courtesy of *Ginka*:
pp. 30, 44, 49, 52, 59, 63. All other photographs were taken by John Tsantes and
Neil Greentree, Arthur M. Sackler Gallery

Library of Congress Cataloging-in-
Publication Data
Cort, Louise Allison, 1944–
A basketmaker in rural Japan / by Louise
Allison Cort and Nakamura Kenji.
p. cm.
Published on the occasion of an exhibition
at the Arthur M. Scakler Gallery of
objects held by the Dept. of
Anthropology, National Museum of
Natural History.
Includes bibliographical references (p.   )
and index. ISBN 0-8348-0336-4
1. Hiroshima, Kazuo, 1915–
—Exhibitions.
2. Basketwork—Japan—Hinokage-
cho—Exhibitions.
3. Basketwork—Washington
(D.C.)—Exhibitions. 4. National Museum
of Natural History (U.S.) Dept. of
Anthropology—Exhibitions
I. Nakamura, Kenji, 1951–
II. Hiroshima, Kazuo, 1915–
III. Arthur M. Sackler Gallery
(Smithsonian Institution) IV. National
Museum of Natural History (U.S.). Dept.
of Anthropology. V. Title
NK3649.55.J34H572 1994
746.41'2'092—dc20
                        94-33582
                          CIP

The paper used in this publication meets
the minimum requirements for the
American National Standard for
Permanence of Paper for Printed Library
Materials, z39.48–1984

Edited by Mary Kay Zuravleff
Designed by Carol Beehler
Composed in Sabon on Apple Macintosh
Printed in 300-line-screen duotone on
100 lb. Mohawk Superfine paper

Contents

Foreword

Milo Cleveland Beach, Director
Arthur M. Sackler Gallery and Freer Gallery of Art

THIS PUBLICATION began with a chance encounter that led to an extraordinary gift to the Smithsonian Institution. In 1982, Sackler associate curator Louise Cort planned and then led, for the Japan Society in New York, a crafts-related tour of southern Japan. Searching for places where the group could see bamboo baskets being made, she wrote to Iiboshi Itsuo, a basketmaker specializing in the bamboo backpacks distinctive to the Hinokage region of Miyazaki Prefecture on the island of Kyushu. Louise Cort's letter brought an unexpected response from Nakamura Kenji, whose family runs a dry goods store in Hinokage. Concerned with preserving the bamboo baskets and other crafts of Hinokage, Mr. Nakamura had begun presenting work by local craftspeople in his store. He hoped that displaying and selling their work would make them better appreciated in their own locale and known to a wider audience. Mr. Nakamura recommended that the Japan Society group visit not only Mr. Iiboshi but also Hiroshima Kazuo, the last man in Hinokage representing the itinerant professional basketmakers who had once served the region.

The Americans' enthusiastic interest inspired Mr. Nakamura to plan for preservation of a permanent record of Hinokage crafts in the United States. He commissioned Mr. Hiroshima to re-create approximately eighty basket forms he had learned during his long career as a basketmaker, and he commissioned carpenters and blacksmiths to replicate the toolbox and tools that Mr. Hiroshima uses. He also ordered a representative selection of backpack baskets from Mr. Iiboshi and gathered samples of other Hinokage crafts, made from bamboo as well as wild vines, rice straw, or wood. He collected a group of older baskets that had survived in local households, and he even gathered representative plastic and metal substitutes that have replaced dwindling bamboo production. Mr. Nakamura's father, Nakamura Kunio, presented the group of 169 items to the National Museum of Natural History in 1988. Five additional items were presented in 1989.

Together with the baskets and other crafts, Mr. Nakamura provided thorough documentation for the nomenclature and use of each basket, together with information on when and how Mr. Hiroshima learned to make it. He also wrote a biographical sketch of Mr. Hiroshima against the background of the historical development of the Hinokage region over the past century. This rich material is the basis for the text of this book, which Louise Cort has translated and augmented with information collected in conversations with Mr. Hiroshima and others during subsequent visits to Hinokage.

Thanks to Mr. Nakamura's energy and vision, the work of Mr. Hiroshima and other Hinokage craftspeople will be preserved in the Department of Anthropology at the Smithsonian's National Museum of Natural History as a highly focused, detailed record of the livelihood of the Hinokage community.

Acknowledgments

Louise Allison Cort

CERTAINLY EXPRESSIONS of thanks must begin with Hiroshima Kazuo, whose thoughtful reflections on his life work as professional basketmaker are the heart of this book. I also give particular thanks to Nakamura Kenji, whose initiative enabled me to meet Mr. Hiroshima. This remarkable pair conceived, created, and documented the collection presented here. Finally, special thanks go to Nakamura Kunio, who encouraged his son's endeavor and sponsored the donation of the collection to the National Museum of Natural History. I treasure the experience of learning about Hinokage baskets from these three exceptional people, and I do not cease to marvel at what they have accomplished.

The Nakamura Collection also represents the work of many other Hinokage craftspeople. Iiboshi Itsuo's handsome backpack baskets first drew me to Hinokage, while Kawashima Tokumatsu's skill at making straw sandals is unforgettable. Kai Katsuyoshi, Kai Akio, Iiboshi Matao, Satō Riichi, Kai Sanji, as well as the late Kai Teruyoshi, Kōrogi Sakai, and Hashimoto Fusae, also contributed their handiwork. Kikuchi Tsuruki, Honda Kunio, Nakamura Keiichirō, Nakayama Kazuo, Kai Chitoshi, and Ōsaka Chiaki donated precious older baskets to the collection.

Numerous other people in the Hinokage area also helped

make the collection possible. Thanks go to all of them, but especially to Fugetsu Restaurant, Himeno Sake Brewery (whose warehouse stored the gathered pieces), and Kunihiro Norinobu, Takachiho office of Nippon Express Co., Ltd.

At the National Museum of Natural History, Paul Taylor, Curator of Asian Ethnology, assisted by Changsu Houchins, supported the museum's acquisition of the Nakamura Collection and later endorsed the Sackler Gallery's publication and exhibition of it. Toshio Saitō of Nippon Express generously arranged a partial donation of the shipping costs.

Preparing this document of the Nakamura Collection was joyful work, involving several return visits to Hinokage. Nakamura Nori graciously wrote a description of the annual cycle of farming and food preservation; her unassuming list of an awesome array of tasks reflects the role played by capable women in maintaining Hinokage farming households. Further instruction came from Kai Kishirō and Shioko, who showed how they still make their own miso and soy sauce, and the Tsushima family, who demonstrated how to make spring equinox dumplings.

The evocative images of Hinokage people and landscapes were commissioned from Dr. Tasaki Tsutomu, a physician in adjacent Takachiho who has won national awards for his photography. Tabuchi Satoru took the photographs of Mr. Hiroshima making a backpack basket.

It was a delight to work on this publication with Sackler Gallery colleagues. Editor Mary Kay Zuravleff pared the prose, while

Carol Beehler's design seems to place the baskets close enough to touch. New photography of all the baskets was accomplished by John Tsantes and Neil Greentree, assisted by registrar Becky Gregson and museum specialist Tim Kirk. For special access to the baskets for photography, our thanks go to Deborah Hull-Walski, collections manager, Greta Hansen, conservator, Felicia Pickering and Susan Crawford, museum specialists, and Deborah Wood, collections specialist, all of the Department of Anthropology, National Museum of Natural History. Karen Sagstetter, editor in chief, arranged for co-publication with Weatherhill, Inc. Lynne Shaner assisted editing and Patricia Condit drew the maps. Stinehour Press bent their superb printing skills toward the project.

Publication of this book coincides with an exhibition, *A Basketmaker in Rural Japan,* held at the Sackler Gallery from 20 November 1994 through 9 July 1995. The Department of Anthropology kindly loaned baskets and tools from the Nakamura Collection, while a Smithsonian Institution Special Exhibition Fund grant supported both the exhibition and the publication. Heartfelt thanks go to all the accomplished Sackler Gallery staff whose assembled skills brought the exhibition into being.

Personally it has been deeply satisfying to focus, through this project, a longstanding interest in basketmaking. For initial guidance in understanding baskets and other tools of Japanese rural life, I am grateful to Kanzaki Noritake and Kudō Kazuyoshi. Finally, I am thankful for Joanna King's introduction to Mr. Iiboshi—the beginning of such a rewarding relationship with Hinokage and its baskets.

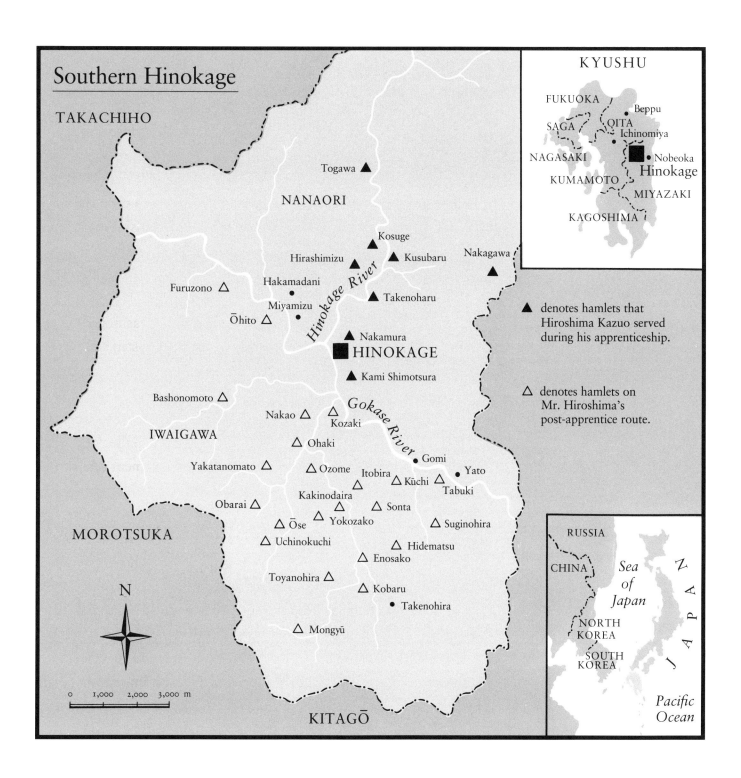

Southern Hinokage

TAKACHIHO

NANAORI

Togawa ▲

Kosuge ▲

Hirashimizu ▲   ▲ Kusubaru   Nakagawa
                                            ▲
Furuzono △   Hakamadani
                  •   ▲ Takenoharu
         Miyamizu
            •
Ōhito △

              ▲ Nakamura
              ■ HINOKAGE

              ▲ Kami Shimotsura

Bashonomoto △

                              Gokase River
Nakao △   △ Kozaki
IWAIGAWA
         △ Ohaki
Yakatanomato △
              △ Ozome   Gomi
                     Itobira   •
                        △ Kūchi   Yato
Obarai △   Kakinodaira   Tabuki   •
              △
         △ Ōse △ Yokozako   △ Sonta
MOROTSUKA
         △ Uchinokuchi   △ Suginohira

                              △ Hidematsu
                    △ Enosako
Toyanohira △
              △ Kobaru
                        • Takenohira

              △ Mongyū

Hinokage River

N

0   1,000   2,000   3,000 m

KITAGŌ

KYUSHU

FUKUOKA
                    • Beppu
SAGA   ŌITA
              • Ichinomiya
NAGASAKI
                    ■
KUMAMOTO   • Nobeoka
              Hinokage
              MIYAZAKI
KAGOSHIMA

▲ denotes hamlets that
  Hiroshima Kazuo served
  during his apprenticeship.

△ denotes hamlets on
  Mr. Hiroshima's
  post-apprentice route.

RUSSIA
                    *Sea
                    of
CHINA   Japan*
                              J
                              A
NORTH   P
KOREA   A
                    N
SOUTH
KOREA
              *Pacific
              Ocean*

Hinokage and Its Baskets

THE MODERN town of Hinokage lies at the northern edge of Miyazaki Prefecture on the island of Kyushu, the southernmost of the four main islands in the Japanese archipelago. Situated well inland from the city of Nobeoka on the Pacific Ocean coast, the town occupies terrain formed by steep-sloped mountains, which range from several hundred to well over a thousand meters above sea level. The Gokase River cuts a deep, V-shaped valley through the region from west to east; the Hinokage River descends swiftly into the Gokase from the north, and smaller streams flow toward it through narrow valleys both north and south of the Gokase.

Inland along the Gokase River from Hinokage lies Takachiho, a setting for mythological events of great significance to Japan. Ninigi-no-mikoto, grandson of Amaterasu, the Sun Goddess, is said to have descended from heaven on a rainbow bridge at Takachiho to found the Japanese nation. According to another myth about the area, Amaterasu, angered by her younger brother's mischief, once hid herself in a cave called Ama-no-iwato, plunging the world into darkness until a goddess's dance provoked merriment among the assembled gods and enticed her out again. That performance is said

Note: All Japanese names in this publication are given in Japanese order, with surname first, followed by given name.

Farm women carrying tools and backpack baskets prepare to work in a newly planted rice paddy.

to be the origin of the sacred masked dances called *kagura;* in appointed households of Takachiho and Hinokage, *kagura* is performed throughout the night from November through February to reenact the myths and bring blessings on the community.

Traces of habitation since Paleolithic times have been found within Hinokage. Later, mountainous Hyuga Province, as Miyazaki Prefecture was known before 1873, provided a secluded refuge for vanquished royalty fleeing the Korean peninsula during the Three Kingdoms period (first to seventh century) and for remnants of the defeated Heike clan in the twelfth century.

The town of Hinokage is a modern administrative creation, drawing together several dozen small settlements that developed at least five centuries ago on the hilltops above the deeply shaded streams and rivers. The homes face south to catch the sunlight, terraced fields line the upper slopes, and the family graves stand in a cluster on household land, rather than on the distant temple grounds. From the seventeenth to the mid-nineteenth century, this region lay within the domain of the warrior family based in Nobeoka Castle. By that time the individual hamlets, consisting of no more than a few dozen households, were consolidated as the villages of Nanaori to the north of the Gokase River and Iwaigawa to the south. In 1951, the two villages merged to form the town of Hinokage, and in 1956, they incorporated Mitate, a village north of Nanaori with a copper and tin mine that had been active as far back as the fifteenth century. In the 1950s the new town grew to 16,199 people (2,653 households); however, the closing of the Mitate mine as well as a general

One of the swift streams that run through Hinokage's narrow valleys.

trend toward depopulation of farming villages throughout Japan has reduced the population steadily to its present level of slightly more than 7,000 inhabitants.

The old administrative center for Nanaori Village was the hilltop community of Miyamizu, which overlooked the meeting place of the Hinokage and Gokase Rivers. After a paved road from Nobeoka was built along the Gokase River's edge at the beginning of this century, people moved down the slopes to the riverbanks and created the modern town. Citizens living there or coming to do errands are constantly crossing the two bridges connecting the three portions of the little town, with its administrative offices, schools, hospital, inns, restaurants, and two sake breweries; its shops for meat, fish, dry goods, hardware, and clothing; and its workshops of a tatami maker, a blacksmith, and a carpenter.

The railroad connecting the town to Nobeoka opened in 1935, replacing travel by riverboat, horsecart, rickshaw, or private taxi—or, for many, by foot. In 1985, the 137-meter-tall Blue Cloud Bridge, the highest bridge in Asia, opened a new route from peak to peak high above the rivers and the town center. This modern bypass, part of the national highway network, has returned long-distance and much local traffic to the mountaintop routes of the past. The town's center is in the process of shifting once again, as merchants relocate along the highway, seeking the patronage of travelers at shops selling local products.

Independent of their nostalgic appeal to tourism, the products of Hinokage are characteristic of the mountainous terrain. A gazetteer of Miyazaki Prefecture from the 1880s gives statistics on the annual produce of Nanaori Village: 200 colts, 30 deer and wild boar, 500 *koku* (1 koku is approximately 5 bushels) of corn, 1,000 *kan* (1 *kan* is equivalent to 3.75 kilograms) of mulberry bark, 15 *koku* of rapeseed (to be pressed for oil), 3,000 *kan* of hemp, 25 *kan* of devil's tongue jelly *(konnyaku)*, 2,000 bales of paper, 50,000 pieces of quince bark, 500 bales of charcoal, 750 *koku* of sake, 30 *koku* of barley liquor *(shōchū)*, 60,000 quail eggs, 1,500 *kan* of *shiitake* mushrooms, and 30 *kan* of dried bamboo shoots.[1]

Even today, farming households in the Hinokage region engage in a range of activities (such as growing rice, cultivating *shiitake* mushrooms, and raising cattle) for income (see "The Annual Work Cycle of a Hinokage Farming Family"). The sustenance for the family combines homegrown and harvested products, many processed at home, with purchased staples. A typical farming establishment consists of the main house (with adjacent rooms for storage and cooking) and the barn (for cattle and, in the past, horses). Around the house grow sweet and astringent persimmon, Asian pear, and citron *(yuzu)* trees. Many households have a space dedicated to sheltering the logs used to raise *shiitake* and a shed for drying the mushrooms. Paddy fields produce both regular rice and glutinous rice *(mochigome)*, for home use and for sale, interplanted with rye in the winter. The fields yield wheat, corn, potatoes, and beans. The vegetable garden produces eggplants, cucumbers, burdock root, pumpkins, Irish potatoes, beans, giant radishes, carrots, Chinese cabbages, and onions. Nearby streams yield varieties of small fish.

Farming families in the mountainous regions gather wild vegetables and bamboo shoots, cultivate tea bushes and chestnut trees, and used to cut hardwood to make their own charcoal. Salt, sugar, rice vinegar, dried sardines, seaweed, ocean fish, and sake—products of other regions or of specialists—have always been purchased.[2]

Lumber has always been important; logs were once floated down to the confluence of the Hinokage and Gokase Rivers, where they were bound into rafts to be floated downriver to Nobeoka. Especially in the interior villages, charcoal-making was a common activity (nos. 66–68) until other fuels replaced charcoal for heating. Since the 1930s, cultivated rows of cedar, cypress, or pine have increasingly replaced the old mixed forests, and bald patches of clear-cut land disfigure the dark green slopes. Groves of chestnut and citron have been expanded with financial encouragement from the town hall. This commercial exploitation of the mountain slopes endangers the once-abundant bamboo groves, which supplied basketmakers but have little economic value in the modern market. (The grove from which Mr. Hiroshima cut the bamboo for the Nakamura Collection was destroyed by the landowner to plant chestnut trees.)

Until recently, bamboo baskets figured in the cultivation, harvesting, and processing of most Hinokage products. Hinokage lies within the forested region of Kyushu, the natural habitat of the mushroom called *shiitake (Lentinus edodes),* which takes its name from the pasania *(shii)* tree on which it often grows. *Shiitake* used to be harvested from the wild, but since the 1920s many Hinokage farmers have cultivated the profitable crop by injecting spawn into

A bamboo grove.

prepared lengths of hardwood logs that are lined up in the shade.[3] (With this process, production has now spread throughout Japan.) Initially they supplied the mushrooms dried (nos. 80, 81, and 83) but unsorted in bulk to wholesalers, who sorted and packaged them. Growers were able to charge a better price by doing the sorting themselves, using a set of bamboo sieves in up to ten graded sizes (nos. 62–65 represent the sizes used most often). By the 1970s the demand for such sieves outstripped Mr. Hiroshima's ability to supply them, and so he provided sieves as models for the Hinokage Agricultural Cooperative to make in plastic (no. 165) and sell to local growers.

In the mountainous interior of Miyazaki Prefecture, the ancient practice of swidden agriculture, whereby hillsides are burned and replanted, survived long after it had vanished elsewhere, because of the difficulty of clearing and leveling enough land to support even a small population. Nonetheless, over centuries of habitation, the steep slopes of the Hinokage region have been gradually cut away into tiers of terraced fields, each propped by a wall of carefully laid boulders, kept free of weeds by hand cutting, and drained by well-maintained channels. The present Hinokage landscape is a monument to the cumulative accomplishment of human effort. Created for this terrain, where farming and harvesting require climbing and descending steep slopes, the distinctive Hinokage backpack basket *(karui),* with wide mouth but narrow base, allows the wearer to maintain balance while transporting heavy loads (nos. 92–103).

The farmers who terraced the slopes created fields in which they planted buckwheat, barley, wheat, rye, millet, Deccan grass, and

Hinokage women pick tea using hip baskets. The woman in back wears a basket woven from plastic strips, a modern replacement for bamboo.

corn. Until recently, the basic starches in the diet of Hinokage residents comprised these grains—made into flour for noodles (wheat *udon* or buckwheat *soba;* no. 53) or steamed buns *(dango),* or cooked together with a little rice (nos. 2, 44, 46, 47, 50, 170, and 171). Although Hinokage households now eat rice daily, in the past it was reserved for festival feasts (no. 41). Some rice could be grown relying upon rainfall, but widespread creation of rice paddies depended upon access to a predictable supply of abundant water. In the 1920s, a system of pipes was laid to carry water from the higher mountain slopes down to paddy fields. To create the paddy fields, farmers had to dig up dry fields, which they did using earth-carrying baskets (nos. 88–90). Such conversion continued until recently, when government policy designed to deal with excess rice production forbade creation of new paddies and even restricted use of existing ones. (The severe rice shortage following the cold summer of 1993 has caused those regulations to be reversed for the short run.)

Another staple crop was taro, which can be left over winter and harvested as needed (no. 45). It was used regularly in soup and, on festivals and special occasions, in the elaborate stew called *nishime,* which also incorporated dried *shiitake,* dried bamboo shoots, devil's tongue, and other vegetables. The root vegetable called devil's tongue *(konnyaku)* grew well in swidden fields. It was processed at home by boiling and pounding in a mortar, and it solidified into a gelatinous mass (no. 53). Bamboo shoots were one of the many vegetables gathered from the wild, using the hip basket (nos. 59–61 and 119) or backpack basket.

A fisherman empties eels from narrow traps into the large container in which he will take them to market.

The deep valleys of Hinokage harbor the cold mists necessary for successful tea production, which expanded into a commercial enterprise in the late nineteenth century. Villagers there processed the tea in the *kamairi* way: they picked the leaves in May, using hip baskets made of bamboo (no. 59) or vine (no. 119), stored them in large baskets (nos. 76–77), steamed them in an iron kettle, spread them out on a bamboo mat (no. 82), and kneaded them into cylinders. The rolled leaves were dried over a charcoal fire before being kneaded once again.[4] Most farming households grew enough tea for their own use, but some specialized in commercial processing, using sieves to sort the leaves into grades of fineness (nos. 48–49).

Another crop that took on commercial importance in the late nineteenth century was the small citron called *yuzu,* used as flavoring in Japanese cooking. Within the region, the fruit had been a source of vinegar, which was stored in bamboo cylinders (no. 108). In recent years merchants have developed a range of commercial products based on *yuzu,* such as jellied sweets and powdered flavorings, to be sold as souvenirs of Hinokage.

Until forty or fifty years ago, Hinokage farmers kept both horses and cattle in their barns. During the winter months, the animals were fed with boiled grain or cut grass. Farmers carried grass from the mountainsides in large backpack baskets meant for lightweight but bulky loads (no. 97), then they chopped and transferred the feed into troughs, scooping it up with large fan-shaped colanders (no. 70). Manure, an important source of fertilizer for the fields, was transported back up the mountainsides in backpack baskets (no. 94) or hemispherical baskets (no. 40). Cattle plowed the fields and paddies, but they also carried heavy loads; for example, cattle hauled wooden casks of sake from the brewery to the shrine for festivals. (Later, sake became available in glass bottles and could be transported by bicycle; nos. 72–74.) Horses, which many households kept until the 1930s, moved heavy loads up and down the mountains or pulled carts used for long-distance transport before the train reached Hinokage. Farmers made special straw shoes for both horses and cows for sure footing on the steep slopes (nos. 127–128). Even today most farming households keep a few cows, breed them, and sell the calves in the spring.

The grains and vegetables grown on the slopes were supplemented by varieties of fish, which used to be abundant in Hinokage's rivers and streams. Catching eels and small fish was a major form of summer play for children, while adult men fished for enjoyment as well as to supply their families with food (nos. 23–26). Local waters yielded shrimp, river crabs, sweetfish, dace, and carp in season (nos. 8–13 and 17–22). Specialists caught and sold these fish for a livelihood. Groups of men living near the rapids of the Gokase River banded together to build weirs with wood and bamboo to trap sweetfish swimming downstream to spawn (nos. 14–16).

While the central town has shops for various foods, many households have continued to make staples such as fermented soybean paste (miso), soy sauce, and pickles. Once, every farmhouse had a storeroom ("miso room") off the kitchen for long-term cold storage of fermented products. Soybean paste is made from barley and

soybeans, salt, and a rice yeast made with store-bought bacterial starter.[5] This paste is the base for the soup served daily with meals (nos. 51–52). Soy sauce is made from a mixture of soybeans, wheat, salt, and rice yeast; the mixture is packed in a flat-bottomed wooden barrel and a bamboo cylinder (no. 54) is pushed through the center. Gradually, liquid from the mixture—soy sauce—seeps into the cylinder.[6] The sauce is ladled out (no. 110) for use as seasoning in clear soups, noodle broth, or stews. Bean curd (tofu) is made from ground cooked soybeans and bittern drained from sea salt stored in a conical basket (nos. 55, 112, and 113).[7]

Until the late nineteenth century, the majority of clothing worn by Hinokage residents was made from hemp, a major product of the region. Women processed the hemp stalks to extract the fiber and, at night, after other work was done, laboriously twisted the lengths end to end to form thread, which they coiled into bamboo baskets (no. 71) until they had enough to warp their looms.[8] (Mr. Hiroshima remembers such a basket among his mother's belongings.) Jackets of purchased cotton were saved for special occasions such as weddings. Some households raised silkworms but only for sale (nos. 7, 78, 79, 84, and 85); silkworm cultivation was more common in adjacent Takachiho. Hemp was also sold commercially and used locally for rope. Thin hemp rope figured in making certain baskets (for holding the horizontal bands of the *karui* backpack basket in place while weaving, or for reinforcing vulnerable areas) until it was replaced by iron wire or plastic rope.

Baskets and other locally made utensils—utilizing wood, rice

A woman in her kitchen.

straw, and wild vines and woods—once served all the life-sustaining and income-producing activities of people in the Hinokage region. With growing commercialization of local products in the late nineteenth century, driven by a need for cash, came increased specialization in basket shapes—and in basketmakers. In recent decades, especially since the end of World War II, old patterns of life, in which the farming households were largely self-sufficient and relied extensively on harvesting from the wild, have been supplanted by closer connection to urban centers and their markets and products. Within Hinokage, a few households still make their own soy sauce ("because it tastes better") but most buy it in bottles at the grocery store. Oil burners have replaced charcoal stoves for drying *shiitake;* frozen fish from the Pacific Ocean supplant local river fish, whose numbers are also reduced by recent problems of pollution and construction of dams. The baskets remembered and still made by Hiroshima Kazuo and other basketmakers in Hinokage offer an opportunity to understand the specificity of baskets to a particular region's geography and economy. Utensils as simple as a length of bamboo stalk for stirring bean curd or as complex as a *shiitake* sieve illustrate how human thought bent to the requirements of tasks of daily life is manifest in the basketmaker's skill.

Notes

1. *Hinokage-chō shi* (History of Hinokage) (Hinokage: Hinokage-chō Yakuba, 1966), 52.

2. Tanaka Kumao et al., eds., *Kikigaki Miyazaki no shokuji* (Oral history of Miyazaki foodways), vol. 45, *Nihon no shoku seikatsu zenshū* (Anthology of Japanese dietary life) (Tokyo: Nōsan Uoson Bunka Kyōkai, 1991), 54–55.

3. The process of *shiitake* cultivation is described in detail in Jane Grigson, *The Mushroom Feast* (Harmondsworth, England: Penguin Books, 1978), 258–300.

4. Tanaka Kumao et al., eds., *Kikigaki Miyazaki no shokuji* (Oral history of Miyazaki foodways), 228.

5. The process of making fermented soybean paste at home is described in William Shurtleff and Akiko Aoyagi, *The Book of Miso* (Berkeley, Calif.: Ten Speed Press, 1976), 185–94.

6. The process of making soy sauce at home is given in Shurtleff and Aoyagi, 184.

7. William Shurtleff and Akiko Aoyagi, *The Book of Tofu* (Hayama City, Kanagawa Prefecture, Japan: Autumn Press, 1975), 271–89.

8. Rural production and use of hemp cloth is discussed in Louise Allison Cort, "The Changing Fortunes of Three Archaic Japanese Textiles," in *Cloth and Human Experience*, edited by Annette B. Weiner and Jane Schneider (Washington, D.C.: Smithsonian Institution Press, 1989), 386–91.

Hiroshima Kazuo A Life in Bamboo

Hiroshima Kazuo was born on 11 January 1915, the fourth child and second son of Hiroshima Utarō and his wife Kaku. The Hiroshima household was one of just six in the hamlet of Mongyū, which lay deep in the mountains at the southern extreme of what was then the village of Iwaigawa. In all, Utarō and Kaku had eight children. Their household of thirteen people, including one grandparent and two unmarried relatives, supported itself by farming.

At the age of three, Kazuo suffered a dislocation of his right hip, which left him with a permanent limp. His parents sought medical help, but their hamlet was a long distance from the nearest doctor, and limited electrification had reached the area only in the previous year. Without access to x-ray equipment, the local doctor could only reassure them: "He won't die from this, but there's nothing I can do to correct it." Much later, when he was twenty, Mr. Hiroshima consulted a doctor in the Nobeoka hospital. X-rays showed that the dislocation would have been easy to correct when the injury occurred, but over the years, muscles had grown around the dislocated bones. Without the money

The nodes of a bamboo stalk may divide it into many separate sections, but in its heart it always stretches in a single line straight toward the sky.

to pay for an operation, Mr. Hiroshima resigned himself to his condition. "If that accident had happened today, fixing it would have been no problem at all."

The nearest elementary school was in the hamlet of Kobaru, a long walk from Mongyū, and Kazuo's lame leg made it impossible for him to attend school. He passed the time at home by catching fish and eels in the river during the summer and trapping birds with a hemp net in the winter. Although he managed to learn how to read sufficiently, his biggest regret in life is that he never learned to write well.

In the 1920s, quite a few men made their living supplying baskets to households in the hamlets of Hinokage (farm women did not engage in the occupation). Some were local residents who made the rounds of nearby villages, receiving room and board from farming households while they made baskets to order. Others were wandering strangers who sold the baskets they made in their encampments in caves or along riverbanks. For the boy left alone while the other children went to school, the occasional visit of an itinerant basketmaker was a welcome diversion. One of Mr. Hiroshima's early memories, from the time he was five or six, concerns a bamboo craftsman named Satō Suketarō, who lived in the adjoining hamlet of Toyanohira (he died around 1972). While Mr. Satō worked, he entertained the children who gathered around him by telling myths and fables or fashioning bamboo toys (nos. 115–18). Mr. Satō was temperamental and a hard drinker, but he could make any sort of bamboo object that was requested. Much later, Mr. Hiroshima incorporated some of Mr. Satō's skills into his own style.

When Kazuo was about ten years old, he met another sort of itinerant basketmaker. Sasaki Hajime came originally from Oita Prefecture and specialized in round-bottomed baskets with "chrysanthemum" bases *(marukago)*, including rice-storage baskets (no. 28), bean-paste sieves (no. 51), and shallow containers *(zaru)*. While moving from hamlet to hamlet in Hinokage, Mr. Sasaki struck up a relationship with a local woman and came to Mongyū, where Kazuo watched him work.

Kazuo knew that he had to make a decision about his future. According to Japanese custom, the eldest son inherited the family land, so under ordinary circumstances he would have been obliged, as a younger son, to leave home. Because of his lame leg, he might have lived out his life as a dependent in the household of one of his siblings, as did the unmarried relatives who lived in his own home, but that prospect was repugnant. Farming, especially in Hinokage terrain, was not a real option. He needed to find another way of making an independent living.

With his parents' encouragement in 1930, at the age of fifteen (by Western method of counting; sixteen by Japanese method), Mr. Hiroshima became an apprentice to a basketmaker. Kudō Masanori, who was twenty-nine, lived in Kusubaru, a hamlet along the Hinokage River within Nanaori Village, on the opposite side of the Gokase River. He was the second or third son of a farming family and so was not in line to inherit land. Moreover, he suffered from a minor weakness of his legs caused by periostitis (inflammation of the connective tissue around the bone), a common disease in Hinokage at that time, for which there was no cure. Around the age of twenty-two, he had taught himself to make baskets and had begun work as a bamboo craftsman. From his family home in Kusubaru, he traveled a circuit of hamlets along the Hinokage River seeking orders for baskets.

When Mr. Hiroshima chose the craft of basketmaking, he knew that he was associating himself with a group of people viewed unfavorably by the farmers who constituted the majority of rural society. Kudō Masanori typified—as does Mr. Hiroshima—one sort of basketmaker, a farmer with a physical disability who turned to the craft when unable to perform more demanding physical labor. Other basketmakers were even less welcome. In interviews with the authors, Mr. Hiroshima explained the status of basketmakers and talked about his profession. "Some baskets were made by wandering people who stayed in caves in the mountains. They weren't allowed to work in the farmyards. They only came to sell finished goods that they had made where they were staying—to hardware stores in the towns or directly to farming households in the villages.

"In Yato, where bamboo was plentiful, there was a big group of such people living on the riverbank in the 1920s. I saw them at a distance but never talked to them. The husband made the baskets and the wife walked around to sell them. They were people without a registered place of residence [seki]." In Japanese society, which centered around farming communities, a registered residence became the basis of social identity beginning in the seventeenth century.

Mr. Hiroshima remained in the formal apprenticeship for two years, living with Mr. Kudō's family in Kusubaru. In spring and autumn, he traveled with his teacher to gather orders for custom-made baskets. He remembers working alongside his teacher until late at night to fill orders in a hurry.

As a self-taught basketmaker, Mr. Kudō made chiefly the basic basket shapes that were most in demand from farmers and that skilled amateurs could also produce—varieties of backpack baskets *(karui)* and hip baskets *(tego)* used for farming, harvesting, and transporting; round, shallow baskets *(shōke)* used for many kitchen and farmyard tasks, including storage baskets for cooked rice, draining baskets for cups and bowls, and simple sieves; and fishing traps, creels, and storage baskets.

Mr. Hiroshima learned the skills for making all these shapes. He began with the round-bottomed bean-paste sieve (no. 51), a simple form that is easy to weave. His training came informally through the process of assisting Mr. Kudō, by splitting the bamboo stalks for his teacher to peel and split finely or by starting the base of a basket to which Mr. Kudō would add the rim, handle, and lid. Only later, when Mr. Hiroshima began working on his own, did he have to figure out the entire process and compose the complete object. "At that point," he remembers, "the customer became more frightening than my teacher."

Kudō Masanori had learned by imitating the work of other basketmakers in the region when customers gave him baskets to repair or copy. In particular, he had tried to replicate the baskets of a craftsman known to everyone simply as Ushi-don ("Uncle Ushi," *don* being the colloquial term of respect equivalent to *san* used for addressing elder men). That itinerant basketmaker was the man whom Mr. Hiroshima came to revere as his own true teacher. "I've never seen work finer than his—perhaps no one *could* do anything better."

Mr. Hiroshima met the man only once, by chance, in 1930, when he was fifteen and Ushi-don was in his sixties. "I was working in the hut by the side of the road that I shared with my teacher in Kusubaru; my teacher was away fishing. Ushi-don happened to come by. A colander *(shōke)* my teacher had made was hanging on the wall. He asked me to show it to him. 'For the work of someone who hasn't learned from a real teacher, it will do.' He implied that it didn't compare to his own work but was acceptable—he praised it.

The rim is the lifeblood of a colander; if it breaks, the basket falls apart.

"Then he added, 'When Masanori comes back, tell him to make a sturdier rim for this basket. The baskets I make aren't wobbly like this.' To prove his point he gave me a colander and a tray *[bara]* that he had made. He left me with that injunction, and I never saw him again. The rim is the lifeblood of a colander; if it breaks, the basket falls apart. My teacher hadn't learned how to make a really good rim. I was just an apprentice; I couldn't dishonor my teacher, but even now I cannot forget that Ushi-don. The wish to be like him—to possess his skill—is with me still. There's no one alive whose work can compare to his."

In the past, the basketmaker's dependence upon his skills for his ability to earn a living created a reluctance to let others see his working processes—if they were copied, he would lose customers. Ushi-don in particular was known as a loner who did not take apprentices. But Mr. Hiroshima learned Ushi-don's skills when he repaired baskets made by the older craftsman. In dismantling the baskets, he saw that Ushi-don had not taken shortcuts even on aspects of construction not visible to the user. "The round baskets he made stayed round; they didn't become oval or weak and fall apart." Finally Mr. Hiroshima discovered how Ushi-don made the rim so that the end of the bamboo wrapping element would not work loose and come out—by tucking the end in the opposite direction from the way the rim had been wrapped, to counteract the torque. Mr. Hiroshima carries on Ushi-don's creed of not scrimping on the details of even the simplest basket—such as the eel trap that inevitably gets washed away in the river currents. He can recognize where a basketmaker cheated on the details, and he considers such baskets "fakes."

Among surviving baskets by Ushi-don are many with beautiful fine weaves, none that are coarsely woven. Mr. Hiroshima heard numerous stories about Ushi-don's meticulousness in selecting raw materials: asked to make some baskets for a household, he might go to the farmer's hillside to cut bamboo and end up declining the work because not a single stalk in the grove was worth using. Flaunting conventions of farming society, which restricted drinking to festivals, Ushi-don liked to drink barley liquor *(shōchū)* before starting work.

He knew that his skills would bring him customers despite his habits.

"For a long time I did not know his full name or where he had ended his life." In the autumn of 1987, in the process of collecting examples of old baskets to donate to the Smithsonian, Mr. Hiroshima and Nakamura Kenji heard from Kikuchi Tsuruki, a blacksmith in the Hinokage hamlet of Ōhito, that Ushi-don's grave was in their family plot because of a distant connection through marriage. "I went at once to pay my respects at the grave." He learned that Ushi-don's full name was Hiraoka Ushimatsu and that he had served in the Russo-Japanese war in 1905. "He was said to have won a medal and some money—but he drank up or gave away all the money." The Kikuchi blacksmith workshop still had and occasionally used eight baskets made by Ushi-don some sixty to eighty years earlier. Mr. Nakamura acquired three (including nos. 3–4) in trade for three new pieces made by Mr. Hiroshima.

Mr. Hiroshima believes that if he could have studied directly with Ushi-don he would have made better baskets. "Not better in terms of appearance, but better in terms of being suited precisely to the need of the user."

In 1931, about a year after beginning his apprenticeship with Kudō Masanori, Mr. Hiroshima heard that the blade tools used by Ushi-don were special pieces made by a skilled blacksmith in Miyaji hamlet, Ichinomiya Town, Kumamoto Prefecture. Mr. Hiroshima immediately placed an order by postcard to the blacksmith, Sasahara Chōhei, even before his teacher could do so. Mr. Hiroshima found that the new tools enabled him to do far more precise work.

At that time, there were two or three blacksmiths working within Hinokage, but they concentrated on farming tools rather than knives. Few Hinokage bamboo craftsmen owned good tools.

Mr. Sasahara specialized exclusively in the sorts of steel blades needed by bamboo craftsmen. The fact that a blacksmith could make a living in such a narrow specialty reflects the numbers of bamboo craftsmen active at the time. In Hinokage alone, about ten basketmakers served the community.

As a descendent of swordsmiths, Mr. Sasahara possessed outstanding blade-making skills that earned him a widespread reputation. He made three different kinds of bamboo-splitting knives, and Mr. Hiroshima always ordered the leaf-shaped blade (see no. 137). Mr. Hiroshima sent for tools from Sasahara Chōhei and his son Ichiji until around 1955, when he received a postcard declining his order and explaining that the workshop was going out of business because of the dwindling demand for bamboo-working tools and the lack of a successor.

Mr. Hiroshima's first order to the Sasahara workshop in 1931 was as follows (see nos. 137–40 and 142):

bamboo-splitting knife, length 6 *sun*: 1 yen 20 sen
tool for binding rims: 20 sen
awl for binding rims: 25 sen
faceting knife: 60 sen
die for weaving strips *(buyose)*, pair of left and
   right blades: 50 sen
trimming blade: 60 sen

At that time, one *masu* (about 1.5 kilograms) of rice cost 30 sen and a *masu* of barley cost 16 sen; 100 sen equal 1 yen.

A printed notice enclosed with the first tools sent from Mr. Sasahara advised that the best source of bamboo-cutting saws was the Usui Foundry in Osaka, which made bow-shaped saws (see no. 144). Mr. Hiroshima placed an order at once and still uses the same brand of saw, which cuts an even edge without splinters.

In 1960, Mr. Hiroshima first ordered some blades from a young Hinokage blacksmith, Kai Teruyoshi. Kai was born into a blacksmithing family in Tsukabaru hamlet of Morotsuka Village, adjacent to Hinokage, in 1932. After graduating from junior high school in 1949, he was apprenticed to a blacksmith; upon completion of his training in 1956, he moved to Hinokage. He specialized in sickles, hatchets, and hoes for farm use but gradually shifted toward parts for construction projects. Until his death in 1991, Mr. Kai supplied Mr. Hiroshima with his basketmaking tools.

In 1987, as Nakamura Kenji was assembling the collection for the Smithsonian, he commissioned Kai Teruyoshi to make a set of tools replicating Mr. Hiroshima's standard assortment. Mr. Kai charged the following (nos. 137–42, respectively):

bamboo-splitting knife: 7,000 yen
tool for binding rims: 3,500 yen
awl for binding rims: 1,000 yen
faceting knife: 1,500 yen
die for weaving strips: 5,000 yen
trimming blade: 4,500 yen

For comparison, in 1987, 1.5 kilograms of rice cost 750 yen and the same amount of barley, 390 yen.

An array of specialized tools, Mr. Hiroshima points out, distinguishes the professional from the farmer who usually makes do with a single all-purpose blade when making his baskets. Tools, coupled with intention and experience, enable the professional to make the best of his raw materials.

Mr. Hiroshima completed his apprenticeship in 1932. There was no formal ceremony to conclude the teacher-student relationship, but Mr. Hiroshima recalls that Kudō Masanori gave him a roll of cloth, which he used to have a shirt made. In appreciation for his training, he worked for room and board for another year. At that point Mr. Kudō made him independent, saying that the apprentice had surpassed the teacher's skills. Thereafter, Mr. Kudō gave up bamboo work and left the area to work in a coal mine in Fukuoka Prefecture, where he was killed in a mine accident at the age of thirty-seven. His career as a bamboo craftsman lasted around ten years.

In the winter months my hands would stiffen. I used to dream of being able to work inside the house.

In 1933 Mr. Hiroshima left Kusubaru and returned to Mongyū to begin his independent career. At first he planned to study in Beppu, in Oita Prefecture—a hotspring town that has been a center for ornamental basketry since the last century—but his family opposed him; knowing he would eventually settle in Mongyū, they contended that such baskets would be of no use in the countryside. And so he took up the standard life of an itinerant basketmaker, gradually building his reputation and his clientele. He lived in his parents' home, but twice each year, in early spring and at the start of the harvest season in early autumn, he was summoned by various hamlets within what is now Hinokage. He might spend up to three months in a hamlet, giving about one week to the work of each interested household. He would sleep in the house and take his meals with the family while filling orders for new baskets, but he worked outside under the broad eaves of the house. "In the winter months my hands would stiffen. I used to dream of being able to work inside the house."

Kudō Masanori had charged by the basket, but Mr. Hiroshima preferred to be paid a fixed amount per day, regardless of the number or kind of baskets he made. He didn't want to contend with complicated calculations that selling by the basket would have entailed, and he never counted the money that he received. During the depths of the economic depression in 1932 and 1933, his daily wage was about 50 sen; in 1935, it was 1 yen 20 sen; in 1941, about 3 yen. He worked from dawn to dusk—in summer, twelve to fourteen hours, in winter, ten hours a day. He took his meals quickly to get the maximum amount of work done each day.

Mr. Hiroshima rarely went to the same household two years in a row; once in three years was typical, since certain basic baskets such as fertilizer backpack baskets wore out in that time span. It was not unusual to make six or seven backpack baskets at a time for one household. Other pieces might last longer if they were well cared for. He often repaired the broken corners of backpack baskets, which were vulnerable where the bamboo bent sharply, the portions of kitchen colanders that had been scorched on the wood-burning stove, and rims that had become unwound.

Occasionally a farmer would decide to cut down a whole mountainside to use the hardwood as charcoal; then Mr. Hiroshima would stay a month or so to use up whatever bamboo had been cleared in the process, making baskets for relatives and neighbors also. Mongyū was a center for charcoal production, and Mr. Hiroshima made many sieves for the charcoal burners (nos. 66–68).

From about 1880 to 1940, a few farming households in Hinokage earned cash by raising silkworms and selling the cocoons to textile mills. Mr. Hiroshima made baskets for this process, which required dozens of sets of flat trays to hold the hungry worms and the mulberry leaves they eat (nos. 78–79 and 84–85).

If a household notified Mr. Hiroshima in advance that they wanted him to work for them, he would go in autumn to cut the bamboo for spring basketmaking; otherwise, someone in the household would cut the bamboo in anticipation of placing an order. Late autumn is the best season for cutting bamboo. Each autumn he cut the bamboo that he would use up to the beginning of the rainy season (in May) the following year. After the rainy season, in late June or early July, he would cut enough to last until autumn. Baskets made during the rainy season were vulnerable to insect infestation, so Mr. Hiroshima concentrated then on fishing baskets, which seldom lasted longer than one season anyway.

Mr. Hiroshima emulates Ushi-don's fastidiousness in choos-

ing his raw materials. "Selecting the bamboo is the most crucial step in making a good basket. Bamboo growing in gravelly soil has the right hardness and flexibility. I look for straight stalks with flat nodes and long segments between the nodes, in order to make weaving strips that are as smooth as possible. Nodes are a nuisance in weaving." The best bamboo to use in basketmaking is three or four years old; it can be distinguished by its shiny green skin. Only a few stalks on a hillside may be suitable. Bamboo can't be cut in the same place two years in a row; three or four years must pass before the next batch of shoots matures.

In the use of the stalks he does select, Mr. Hiroshima is never miserly. A bamboo stalk is made up of the green skin *(kawa)* and the creamy white flesh *(mi)*. The flesh is soft: bugs can easily attack it, and it wears out quickly. But there's much more flesh than skin in a stalk, and some basketmakers cut weaving strips from the flesh to make a better profit from their materials. Mr. Hiroshima trims the excess flesh away from the skin and burns it; he weaves only with strips bearing skin. "This is not a profession to get rich in," he laughs.

"The straightest part of the stalk is located just below a branch. I use that part for the rim strips. Making the rim is the key; it holds the finished basket together." He wraps the rim of a round, shallow *shōke* basket six times for sturdiness. "Other weaving strands can be taken from any part of the bamboo—I have learned how to work with them to weave a good, even basket."

The basketmaker's skill is pitted against the nature of the

Mr. Hiroshima uses a cross-shaped tool to split a bamboo stalk into quarters, beginning at the top and working toward the root.

material. Mr. Hiroshima concedes, "Bamboo is honest—it shows everything," including the bamboo worker's proficiency or lack of it.

In 1935, a friend encouraged Mr. Hiroshima to take on as his first apprentice Morita Tomio, a seventeen-year-old from Morotsuka Village, who stayed for a year, then quit. "He was determined, but he just couldn't learn," Mr. Hiroshima remembers.

By the summer of 1937, Japan was at war with China. Mr. Hiroshima recalls that children in the villages he visited asked him to make toy antiaircraft guns out of bamboo (nos. 116–117).

In 1939, Mayor Fukuda of Nanaori Village (later incorporated into Hinokage) conceived a plan for rehabilitating local men who had been injured in the war by training them to make baskets. He summoned a basketmaker from Kagoshima Prefecture to train about twenty disabled men, and Mr. Hiroshima was invited to join the class. The project did not last long. Mr. Hiroshima learned how to make flower baskets and other display pieces that were the specialty of the Kagoshima basketmaker, but today he has forgotten those techniques completely. The most important benefit of this encounter was seeing the Kagoshima specialist use an improved die for standardizing the width of the weaving strips (no. 141). Mr. Hiroshima at once ordered one from the foundry that supplied parts to the electric power plant, at a cost of 1 yen 20 sen.

The weaving strip is the final result of processing the stalk of bamboo, which is about ten meters long. Mr. Hiroshima uses his bamboo-splitting knife to cut the stalk vertically in half, in quarters, then progressively thinner until he has weaving strips *(higo)* just a few millimeters wide, from which he trims the flesh—not just once but several times—to form thin green bands of bamboo skin. He sets the gauge on the die and runs all the strips through it to assure absolute uniformity of width.

"The size of the *higo* is the key to making a good basket—it must match the type of basket being made." Varying the size of the weaving strip in a single basket is also required for making rounded forms; narrow strips are used to weave the curved portions. The hardest baskets to weave are those such as the rice-rinsing colander (no. 41) and the storage basket for cooked rice (nos. 1, 27, and 28). These require a smooth interior surface on which grains of rice will not catch, so all the nodes must lie on the outside.

In 1943, during the war, Mr. Hiroshima was drafted and sent to a Nobeoka bamboo workshop to manufacture essential containers that were in short supply. He worked at the shop of Satō Shin'ichi, receiving room and board as well as a daily wage. In the Satō workshop, four or five professional basketmakers worked alongside fifteen women volunteers. "City basketmakers are different," Mr. Hiroshima noted, "they use different tools." From those experienced basketmakers, who were in their forties, Mr. Hiroshima learned the repertory of shapes that served the urban market along with the tools and techniques peculiar to their manufacture. For example, the shop supplied sturdy square-sided baskets, regularly used in Nobeoka vegetable and fish markets, to a rayon factory for holding the fiber at various stages of processing (nos. 72–74); the key to their successful production was a trimming blade (no. 142) for thinning the strips where they were to bend at the corners. After the war he produced such baskets in Hinokage for use as bicycle delivery baskets. The Satō workshop made a wide assortment of baskets for cooking in field kitchens (nos. 56–58) and for construction use (especially carrying fans for moving earth, like no. 88, and colanders).

Mr. Hiroshima remained on at the Satō workshop for some months after the war ended, helping to fill the endless orders for all sorts of utilitarian baskets to replenish households, shops, and factories devastated by the war. In his own business as late as 1950, he could sell as many bean-paste sieves, drainers, and colanders as he could make.

In 1946, Mr. Hiroshima's older sister, Mrs. Yamamoto, asked him to come live with her in Unama hamlet within Kitagō Village, adjoining Hinokage to the south across the pass from Mongyū. At the urging of his sister and her husband, he took on their son Hiroshi (age fifteen) as an apprentice, but the boy quit after a year, tempted by possibilities of more lucrative work as the country began to recover from the war. While living and working in Unama, Mr. Hiroshima learned how to make bamboo baskets used in the hamlets within Kitagō Village. These included distinctive shapes of eel baskets (no. 9) and backpack baskets (nos. 104–6), and the pair of baskets carried on a shoulder pole that was the most general means of transporting goods (no. 91). The broad-bottomed Unama backpack baskets, equivalent in function to the *karui* used in Hinokage, as well as the shoulder-pole baskets, were suited to the gentler terrain.

Mr. Hiroshima interlaces weaving strips to form the base of a backpack basket.

In 1947, Mr. Hiroshima married Satō Kikuyo, who came from a hamlet in Takachiho. He was thirty-two years old; she was twenty-eight. (The couple has one son, Hitoku, who is an administrator at a college in Osaka.) The following year, they moved from Unama back to Hinokage—not to Mongyū but to the riverside hamlet of Gomi on the Gokase River.

That move—and the many changes brought about in Japan by the war—effectively brought to a close Mr. Hiroshima's old pattern of work as an itinerant craftsman. From then on, he worked in one place, and people came to him with their orders. Symbolically, he acquired a wooden toolbox to replace the backpack basket in which he had formerly transported his tools.

In Gomi, which supported an active fishing industry, orders for fishing baskets became a major part of Mr. Hiroshima's business. Sasaki Hajime, one of the basketmakers he had met as a child, had settled in the adjacent hamlet of Yato. Mr. Sasaki, who died around 1977, was famous for his square-shouldered creels (baskets worn by fishermen to collect their catch), and from him Mr. Hiroshima learned special modifications for the type of creel that became one of his most popular specialties (no. 12). Mr. Hiroshima also learned how to weave many of the traps and creels made by the fishermen themselves, including traps for dace (no. 19) and river crabs (nos. 17 and 20) and baskets for holding live eels and fish (nos. 14–16), and he devised

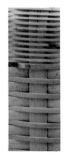

I was at my wit's end looking after those apprentices. Teaching is difficult, and I struggled. Despite the struggle I was unable to pass along the skills I had mastered to someone else.

ways to improve upon them (for example, no. 21, an improved trap for river crabs).

In 1951, Mr. Hiroshima contracted with the Kawano Bait and Tackle Store in Nobeoka to provide one to two hundred woven eel traps (no. 24) to the store each year. The main customers for these simple traps were children, but orders declined as pollution reduced the number of eels in the river.

While in Gomi, Mr. Hiroshima took on three more apprentices. Niina Masaharu, from Daira hamlet in Hinokage, joined him in 1953 and trained for about two years. He was promising; however, he received an opportunity to marry into a farming family as an adopted son and so inherit land. Mr. Hiroshima still regrets that he could not train him completely. Kai Takeyoshi came by bicycle from Ōhito hamlet in 1954 but gave up after two years because of family difficulties. In 1955, Nakasaki Shizuyoshi walked from his home in Kūchi in Hinokage; he left his apprenticeship after two years and now works as a shop clerk in Miyazaki City.

Mr. Hiroshima regrets that none of the five young men who became his apprentices had the ambition to absorb his skills and surpass them in their own work. One reason was the visible decline in demand for bamboo baskets, but he also failed to meet a youth who was determined or able to learn this unglamorous, exacting work. "I was at my wit's end looking after those apprentices. Teaching is difficult, and I struggled. Despite the struggle I was unable to pass along the skills I had mastered to someone else." Most of Mr. Hiroshima's apprentices were around twenty, at an age when they

tended to remember the theory rather than learn by execution. "In order to become a craftsman, you should start an apprenticeship by the age of fifteen, when you absorb skills without thinking too much. It's essential to watch the process, then imitate it, gradually become adept, and accumulate your own distinctive skills. It's through this process that the work becomes enjoyable."

During the 1950s, Mr. Hiroshima made large quantities of sieves and winnows for the *shiitake* wholesaling firms Sugimoto and Kawasaki. He taught himself how to make the sieve; it is not an easy shape, requiring special tools to space the mesh and hold it in place (nos. 154 and 156). He improved upon the existing sieve, and the plastic version presently in use is based on his bamboo prototype.

In 1959, Mr. and Mrs. Hiroshima moved from Gomi down-river to Yato, a prosperous center for lumbering, and the location of both a mine and a dam that created good fishing. Moreover, the area was known for abundant bamboo, and the basketmaker Sasaki Hajime lived there. The Hiroshimas still live today on the single main strcct of the town, between the Gokase River and the railroad tracks. A green awning bearing the shop name "Takehiroya" (incorporating the characters for "bamboo" and part of Hiroshima) shades the entrance to the candy shop that Mrs. Hiroshima operates, next door to her husband's workshop and in front of their residence. Mr. Hiroshima sits to work in a well cut into the wooden floor. A window at his back gives light, and one opposite him looks out on the street. Customers open the sliding door to ask, "Can you make me another one of these?" The workshop is too small to accommodate

To make the body of a backpack basket, Mr. Hiroshima interlaces the weaving strips around horizontal bands.

the lengths of bamboo with which he weaves, so he cut an opening beneath the floor of the candy shop to his left and a hole in the wall to his right. The weaving strips, therefore, run the length of both shops and extend into the alley. He stores bamboo for immediate use in a yard behind the shop and additional supplies on the grounds of the village shrine.

From the end of the war until about 1965, orders for bamboo utensils came virtually on a daily basis, so many that Mr. Hiroshima could not fill them all. In addition to orders for fishing and kitchen baskets, Mr. Hiroshima also made large quantities of backpack baskets for carrying gravel (no. 95), earth-moving fans (no. 88), and related shapes for use by construction companies. By around 1970, however, the use of containers made of plastic and other synthetic materials spread from urban centers to Hinokage, and the percentage of bamboo utensils decreased year by year.

In 1975, Mr. Hiroshima became acquainted with a younger basketmaker, Iiboshi Itsuo, who was born in 1928 and lived in Shiiya hamlet in Hinokage. Mr. Hiroshima learned from him how to make backpack baskets *(karui)*. Mr. Iiboshi typifies the postwar pattern of basketmaking in rural Japan. His main income comes from raising and processing *shiitake,* and in his free time he specializes in making the distinctive Hinokage backpack shape, which he has gradually modified to an elegant, tapered form designed to catch the eye of tourists rather than to be used. (According to Mr. Hiroshima, the bottom is too narrow.) With the reduction in orders for bamboo utensils and the growth of tourism in Hinokage and Takachiho, Mr.

Hiroshima anticipated that he could make a living concentrating on *karui* and fashioning miniature versions for sale as souvenirs. He learned how to make the braided rice-straw straps (even though they were not strictly part of basketmaking), so that he could present a complete product.

Mr. Hiroshima was working in that manner in 1978, when Nakamura Kenji first called on him. Son of the owner of the Nakamura Rice Store in the center of Hinokage, Mr. Nakamura had become interested in the crafts of his native region after returning from college and a year working in a company in Nagoya. Mr. Nakamura was surprised when he asked Mr. Hiroshima about *karui* and was told that they were not difficult baskets to make, not a challenge to a professional basketmaker. The young businessman had to visit three times before Mr. Hiroshima took him seriously and agreed to make some baskets for display and sale in the store. Mr. Nakamura told him, "Make whatever you know how to do. You're the only one who can do it now."

This acquaintance revitalized Mr. Hiroshima's enthusiasm for his work. At Mr. Nakamura's request, he began to produce the complete repertory of objects that he had learned during his career—some eighty different shapes. When they went on display in 1979 at the Nakamura store, tourists did buy them, but local people were also delighted to find a renewed source of familiar shapes. (Amateur basketmakers are also dwindling in numbers. The last generation is in their sixties and seventies, and younger men feel that they have neither the time nor the patience to sit and do such work.)

Mr. Hiroshima and Nakamura Kenji paid a visit to the bamboo craftsmen of Beppu City in Oita Prefecture. Mr. Hiroshima wanted to test the wisdom of his decision, made forty years earlier, not to learn those skills. While he admired the work of some of the master basketmakers, he also noticed the impersonal nature of the transactions, mediated by wholesalers and retailers, between the mass-producers of baskets and the nameless tourists.

In November 1981, the square-shouldered creel (no. 12) that Mr. Hiroshima submitted to the twenty-third national juried exhibition sponsored by the Japan Folk Crafts Association in Osaka won a prize for outstanding craftsmanship. In a newspaper interview, Mr. Hiroshima remarked about the award: "I didn't make that basket especially as 'folk craft.' I'm the same person I've always been—I make what I know. There are people who think that, just because I'm a bamboo craftsman, I can make anything and everything from bamboo. That's a big problem."

The display in the Nakamura store caught the eye of the president of UMK Miyazaki Television, Kuroki Shigeo, when he was visiting Hinokage. Consequently, during the autumn of 1981, a young director, Miroku Takeshi, and cameraman Bōno Takaomi spent several weeks filming Mr. Hiroshima at work and recording his thoughts about the profession of basketmaker. The program, "Heart of Japan: Living through Bamboo," premiered as a special New Year program in January 1982.

Mr. Nakamura had acquired a display of more than sixty varieties of baskets, which were hanging on the walls and above the shelves in the store in May 1982, when Louise Cort was leading a group through Hinokage to see bamboo basket production. The thirty members of this tour, sponsored by the Japan Society of New York, were focusing specifically on the crafts of southern Japan. During two days closely orchestrated by Nakamura Kenji, the group saw Iiboshi Itsuo make a *karui* and were taught by Mr. Hiroshima how to weave an eel trap. They also watched Mr. Nakamura's neighbor, eighty-two-year-old Kawashima Tokumatsu, weave varieties of rice-straw sandals, and they sampled local food and liquor.

In 1983, Nakamura Kenji began to develop plans in consultation with Louise Cort for sending a collection of Mr. Hiroshima's baskets and related materials to the National Museum of Natural History at the Smithsonian Institution. Impressed by the interest shown by the Japan Society group, Mr. Nakamura felt that a wider American audience should be introduced to traditional baskets of Japan and the circumstances under which they were made.

A craftsman's proudest moment is when the customer likes what has been made and is happy to have it.

In 1984, Mr. Hiroshima received official recognition from Miyazaki Prefecture as a "Maker of Traditional Crafts" *(dentō kōgei shi)* for his work as a bamboo craftsman; in addition, together with Iiboshi Itsuo, he was acknowledged for production of backpack baskets *(karui)*.[1]

Louise Cort revisited Hinokage in November 1985, and a decision was made to send examples of bamboo crafts to the Smithsonian as a gift from Nakamura Kenji's father, Nakamura

Kunio. Eventually, the collection encompassed 174 items, including tools and related objects. Two years were planned for the completion of the baskets. Mr. Hiroshima looked upon the work as a summary of all that he had accomplished in some sixty years as a bamboo craftsman. He remarked to Nakamura Kenji, "I've never thought that my bamboo work was better than anyone else's. I can remember when there were any number of people doing better work than I can. The purpose of this project is to thank the Japan Society visitors and promote 'person-to-person diplomacy.'"

That same month, he cut the bamboo to use for the baskets for which he had been commissioned; on an auspicious day in December 1985 he began the work.

Mr. Hiroshima refused all local orders to devote himself to the preparation of the baskets. Nakamura Kenji observed: "Mr. Hiroshima doesn't know the meaning of Sunday. Unless he is called away by an urgent errand, he can always be found sitting in his workshop. He feels a tremendous responsibility toward this work. Sometime he calls me up, saying he wants to see pieces he made for me earlier, to refresh his memory." But his pace had slowed, and he worked only four or five hours a day, rather than the morning to evening schedule he had maintained for decades. "It helps to be receiving my pension," he acknowledged.

Mr. Nakamura also decided to order nine backpack baskets *(karui)* from Iiboshi Itsuo, who selected bamboo for the pieces that autumn. Yato carpenter Kai Sanji, born 1922, completed a replica of the toolbox that Mr. Hiroshima has used since 1941 (no. 151), and

To protect the narrow base of a backpack basket, Mr. Hiroshima inserts the pointed end of a thick bamboo strip into one side of the basket, bends the strip across the base, and secures the other end in the opposite side.

in January and February of 1987, Hinokage blacksmith Kai Teruyoshi made a complete set of forged steel tools for bamboo-working, modeled after the set that Mr. Hiroshima uses (nos. 137–43).

After a long spell of trouble with rheumatism aggravated by the unusually cold winter, Mr. Hiroshima was able to begin work again in March 1987. He continued through April and May, stopped for the rainy season when any baskets were likely to become infested with insects, and resumed in September. By November, he had completed all the baskets.

Meanwhile, in August 1987, Kawashima Tokumatsu made twenty pairs of straw sandals representing six different types of footgear (nos. 123–28), including sandals for horses and cattle. That autumn, Iiboshi Itsuo made his *karui*. The mat maker Satō Riichi made six miniature *tatami,* conceived as stands for displaying the baskets (no. 132). Nakamura Kenji prepared documentation of the collection, which was delivered to the Smithsonian in May 1989. In July 1989, Nakamura Kenji sent two additional baskets and three tools (nos. 170–74).

In November 1992, Mr. Hiroshima received a Ministry of Labor award as an "Outstanding Contemporary Craftsman" *(gendai no meikō).* After a trip to Tokyo, accompanied by his son and Nakamura Kenji, where he received the award and toured the Imperial Palace with other recipients, he returned to celebrations in Hinokage and Yato. He was invited to speak to the students at Yato Junior High School, where he was pleased to talk to young people about his life work. And, for the first time in many years, all eight brothers and sisters gathered at the family home in Mongyū to celebrate the award and visit their parents' grave.

Mr. Hiroshima's bamboo-crafting skills, as embodied in his pieces in the Nakamura Collection, incorporate what he learned not only during his apprenticeship but also from three basketmakers (Satō Suketarō, Ushi-don, and Sasaki Hajime) he encountered among the many itinerant professional bamboo craftsmen active in the Hinokage area from the 1870s to the 1930s. He absorbed their skills, made them his own, and amplified upon them. Mr. Hiroshima's repertoire also includes shapes that he learned from Iiboshi Itsuo and other amateur basketmakers—farmers in Hinokage and the surrounding region who piece together rough baskets as tools for their own farming practices. Most of his products were essential to the livelihoods of people living in the Hinokage region. As a result, Mr. Hiroshima's baskets embody all the aspects of bamboo basketry production in Hinokage during the past century.

Hinokage baskets in themselves incorporate forms also found elsewhere in Kyushu and introduced to the area by wandering basketmakers. Some scholars suggest that the unique shape and weave structure of the Hinokage *karui* relate it to baskets from Southeast Asia.[2] This broader geographical comparison is beyond the scope of this study but deserves to be done.

Of the eighty-three basket types prepared by Mr. Hiroshima for the Nakamura Collection, about half the shapes are still in use in Hinokage for the same purposes; the other half are now obsolete as the result of changes in livelihood and manufacturing. Many were made quickly and in quantity, with the expectation that a given basket would wear out shortly with rough use in its intended function. As indicated by the award Mr. Hiroshima received from the Japan Folk Crafts Association in Osaka, some of those baskets are now viewed—irrespective of their original functions—as beautiful craft items and are eagerly sought by urban collectors. Nakamura Kenji occasionally receives telephone calls from people who have seen an article about Mr. Hiroshima's baskets and are eager to acquire one at any price; he refuses such orders. Other baskets did not appeal visually to collectors and have been forgotten. Both types of baskets have importance as reference materials for the study of Hinokage culture, and both are included in the Nakamura Collection.

The world of rural Japanese craftspeople has been presented to English speakers largely through the Japanese Folk Craft Movement, which began in the 1920s under the guidance of the intellectual connoisseur Yanagi Sōetsu (1889–1961).[3] Rural crafts, classified by Mr. Yanagi's invented term as *mingei* ("popular art"), were characterized for most Americans by the title of Mr. Yanagi's influential collection of essays published in English as *The Unknown Craftsman*.[4] As Mr. Hiroshima's career demonstrates, however, the sentimental notion that the maker of crafts used in rural communities was "unknown" was true only for the urban collectors of the Folk Craft Movement.

Mr. Hiroshima almost always made baskets to order; therefore, he knew who would be using each basket and how it would be

Mr. Hiroshima attaches plaited straw straps to finished backpack baskets.

used. He adjusted the basket to the specifications and the physical size of the user. An example is the small backpack used to carry working tools and lunch into the forest: this *karui* was made to be no wider than the wearer's shoulders so that it would not brush against the trees on the narrow mountain paths.

The personal relationship between maker and user did not end with the sale of the basket but would continue for years: the customer would either, when ordering a replacement, let him know how the basket had worked—or not come back. "A craftsman's proudest moment is when the customer likes what has been made and is happy to have it." In the 1930s, when Mr. Hiroshima was working in the old pattern of itinerant basketmaker, going from village to village to make baskets to order, the personal relationship between customer and craftsman extended to community appraisal of the basketmaker's skills and character. Only a craftsman "known" for his dependable skills would be summoned to the hamlets year after year; only a person of reliable behavior and morality would be allowed to work under the eaves of the house and eat and lodge with the family whose baskets he was supplying.

Since the 1950s, Japanese craftspeople have also been presented to the Japanese and Western public through the Living National Treasures program, designated by the Agency for Cultural Affairs of the Ministry of Education. The discussion of craftspeople honored with this designation usually focuses on lineage and style—which generation the artist represents in an established old family workshop, what prizes he or she has won. Mr. Hiroshima's discussion of his career concentrates on more basic issues—what skills the rural craftsman (*shokunin*, literally "person with a saleable skill") had to know to make a living. Mr. Hiroshima tells the events of his life in terms of what he learned, where or from whom, to improve his skills: a way of wrapping a rim, a better tool for a particular job. His career is the cumulative result of steady efforts to improve upon his saleable skills.

Focusing throughout his career on the functions of his products, Mr. Hiroshima has refined his skills in order to make baskets that perform their jobs better. Beauty can be seen—in the fineness of the weaving strips, the evenness of the weave, the meticulous finishing of the rim—but it is a secondary result of the attention to usefulness and durability.

Mr. Hiroshima's conversation returns time and time again to the pain of his lifelong association with an occupation that was looked down upon by the farming community. "It saddens me that bamboo work is done only by ill people, handicapped people, and people disdained by the rest of society. Shōno Shōunsai of Beppu, who was the first bamboo craftsman to become a Living National Treasure, said himself, 'I'm just doing this disdained bamboo work, but I managed to raise it to the level of craft.' When I learned that he said that, although I cannot compare my work to his by any means, I felt as though his honor had honored me as well. It was the same

Making a good basket is more like a form of prayer. When I'm working I keep telling myself, "Do it well, do it well." I want to make something that will please the person who uses it and suit that person's needs.

for blacksmiths and stone carvers and bucket makers—they were all despised for the work they did. But someone like a carpenter can rise in the modern world by going to work for a construction company. Bamboo ends here—there's no further use for it. That's sad."

In recent years, with an established workshop and, now, a government pension relieving him of the daily pressure to earn a living, Mr. Hiroshima has had time to reflect on the process of his craft. "Making a good basket is not a process of *thinking* about what to do. It's more like a form of prayer. When I'm working I keep telling myself, 'Do it well, do it well.' I want to make something that will please the person who uses it and suit that person's needs. And I just try to do work that I can be satisfied with.

"Bamboo craft has continued for three hundred, four hundred years. It's intolerable to think that it will end with my generation. Somewhere, somehow, a seedling will sprout again. In anticipation of that day, so that the skill won't be forgotten, with the time remaining to me I want to make as many more baskets as I can."

From time to time Nakamura Kenji receives a telephone call from Mr. Hiroshima, who announces: "I've located some excellent bamboo and I'm going to work. Isn't that wonderful!"

Notes

1. The awards are documented in *Waga machi no meikō* (Outstanding artisans of our community), (Miyazaki: Miyazaki-ken Ginōshi-kai Rengōkai, 1993).

2. Kudō Kazuyoshi, *Japanese Bamboo Baskets* (Tokyo, New York, and San Francisco: Kodansha International, 1980), 71, and Kudō, *Kurashi no naka no take to wara* (Bamboo and straw in everyday life) (Tokyo: Gyōsei, 1982), 126–27. In June 1994, Louise Cort saw related basket forms in Zhejiang Province, China.

3. The Folk Craft Movement is described briefly in Victor Hauge and Takako Hauge, *Folk Traditions in Japanese Art* (Washington, D.C.: International Exhibitions Foundation, 1978), 14–15, and analyzed at length in Brian Moeran, *Lost Innocence: Folk Craft Potters of Onta, Japan* (Berkeley: University of California Press, 1984).

4. Yanagi Sōetsu, *The Unknown Craftsman*, adapted by Bernard Leach (Tokyo and Palo Alto, California: Kodansha International, 1972).

Catalogue

THE BAMBOO BASKETS and related material in this catalogue are all part of the Nakamura Kunio Collection in the Department of Anthropology, National Museum of Natural History, Smithsonian Institution. Unless otherwise stated, all baskets are the gift of Nakamura Kunio.

These objects are assigned the accession number 380491, followed by the serial number used here. Thus, the first basket in this catalogue is listed in museum records as 380491.1, the second is 380491.2, and so forth. Occasionally, more than one example of an object is included, necessitating a number after a second decimal point; thus, there are two trays for raising silkworms, 380491.7.1 and 380491.7.2. With a few exceptions, only one example of each catalogue number is illustrated.

In Japanese, the initial consonant of a word may change when that word is combined with another; for example, the combinatory form of the *shōke* colander is *jōke*, as in a triangular colander *(sankakujōke)* or a rectangular one *(shikakujōke)*. Likewise, the combinatory form of the *karui* backpack basket is *garui*, and that of *take*, which means "bamboo," is *dake*.

Object measurements are given in centimeters as length by width by height.

Antique Baskets

THESE BASKETS survived in Hinokage households until they were collected for donation to the Smithsonian. Although some of them had been set aside after households ceased the activities (such as raising silkworms) for which the baskets were required, others were still being used. The chaff sieve employed as a charcoal sieve in a blacksmith's workshop (no. 3) illustrates the flexibility of basic basket types. Owners of baskets that had become weakened or damaged might extend the baskets' usefulness by covering them with tough paper called *shibugami*, made from mulberry fiber and strengthened with coatings of fermented persimmon pulp, or *kakishibu* (nos. 5–6). The paper was made in hamlets in adjoining Morotsuka Village and sold in large sheets, which villagers also used as ground covers until plastic sheets became available.

Some baskets had been in use so long—over several generations—that the names of their makers had been forgotten. But three examples (nos. 2–4) were still remembered as the work of Hiraoka Ushimatsu, known as Ushi-don, an itinerant basketmaker active in Hinokage in the early twentieth century. His baskets stand out for their meticulous workmanship, starting with the extreme fineness and evenness of the weaving strips *(higo)*. While Mr. Hiroshima did not apprentice with him and in fact met him only once, he views Ushi-don as his true teacher because of what he has learned wordlessly by studying surviving examples of Ushi-don's work.

1 Storage basket for cooked rice

(meshi kago)
Maker unknown, ca. 1930
42 X 42 X 40
Gift of Nakamura Keiichirō,
Miyamizu, Hinokage

In warm weather, cooked rice was stored in this basket, which was hung up high to catch cool breezes that helped keep the rice from spoiling; in winter, it would hold glutinous rice cakes *(mochi)*. Throughout the year, the basket was used as general storage for cooked food and leftovers, to be hung out of reach of household cats.

2 Sieve for crushed corn kernels

(kozane tōshi)
Made by Hiraoka Ushimatsu, ca. 1910–30
45 X 45 X 10
Gift of Nakayama Kazuo,
Hakamadani, Hinokage

A farming family used this sieve to sift pulverized kernels of corn *(tōkibi)* that were to be cooked together with rice. Ushi-don (Hiraoka Ushimatsu) made the sieve at Mr. Nakayama's family home.

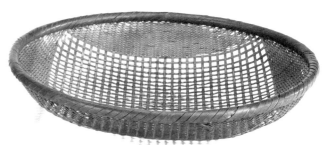

2, 3

3 Chaff sieve

(momi tōshi)
Made by Hiraoka Ushimatsu, ca. 1910–30
58 X 58 X 10
Gift of Kikuchi Tsuruki, Ōhito, Hinokage

Ordinarily used for separating chaff from husked rice or other grain, this sieve was made at Mr. Kikuchi's family home by Ushi-don (Hiraoka Ushimatsu). The Kikuchi family business was blacksmithing, and they used this basket for sifting charcoal. This example illustrates the versatility of many basket shapes, which are named according to their most typical use but can be adapted to other purposes.

1

4 Tray

(bara)
Made by Hiraoka Ushimatsu
ca. 1910–30
74 X 74 X 10
Gift of Kikuchi Tsuruki, Ōhito,
Hinokage

This tray functioned as a shallow
wooden tub (compare no. 34). Made
at Mr. Kikuchi's family home by
Ushi-don (Hiraoka Ushimatsu), it was
used until around 1975.

5, 6

6 Paper-covered basket

(harijōke)
Maker and date unknown
45 X 45 X 10
Gift of Honda Kunio, Kūchi,
Hinokage

Used to hold grain or dried foodstuffs,
this container was given a new function when someone in the Honda
household covered an old dish-drain-
ing basket *(chawan kago)* with mulberry paper soaked in fermented persimmon pulp.

7.1–2 Trays for raising silkworms

(kaiko bara)
Maker unknown, ca. 1890
97 X 61 X 5
Gift of Kai Chitoshi, Mitai,
Takachiho

In the Kai household, silkworms and
the mulberry leaves they fed on were
placed on netting stretched over a
wooden frame; trays like these were
slid beneath the netting to collect the
silkworm feces. Racks of shelves held
many layers of netting and trays
(compare nos. 84–85). The Kai household used the trays from about 1890
until the 1920s, when they stopped
raising silkworms.

4

5 Paper-covered basket

(harijōke)
Maker and date unknown
59 X 59 X 10
Gift of Honda Kunio, Kūchi,
Hinokage

This container for grain or dried foodstuffs was prepared at Mr. Honda's
home by covering a worn-out fertilizer basket *(koejōke)* with strong mulberry paper soaked in fermented persimmon pulp; the paper created a
smooth surface over the rough weave
of the basket and patched any holes.

7.1

Fishing Baskets

AS A BOY in the hamlet of Mongyū, Hiroshima Kazuo spent his summer days catching fish in a nearby stream. In Hinokage, fishing was an amusement for children; adult men fished to supply food for their families and earn income, either occasionally or on a full-time basis. This was especially true for people living in the hamlets lining the Gokase River.

Many boys and men knew how to construct the basic range of bamboo traps and creels, although professional basketmakers also made them to order. Mr. Hiroshima learned the standard shapes (such as eel traps) during his apprenticeship with Kudō Masanori, who served villages along the Hinokage River. When Mr. Hiroshima took up residence on the banks of the Gokase River in 1948 (first in Gomi, then Yato), he began making more complex basket shapes to trap and hold fish living in the wide, swift river. He also began weaving larger sizes to satisfy professional fishermen, who endeavor to catch quantities of fish as efficiently as possible. Using his specialized skills and tools, he improved upon the basic shapes through stronger construction and modification of details. In recent years, however, the fish population in the Gokase River has been reduced severely through pollution from sewer systems emptying directly into the river, runoff from fertilizers and insecticides, and construction of dams.

8, 9

8 Basket for holding live eels
(unagi hogo)
Made by Hiroshima Kazuo, 1986
34 X 34 X 22

Fishermen would transfer eels caught in traps (nos. 24–26) to this type of basket, which was used on the Gokase River for keeping eels alive on the way to market. The deep, close-fitting lid prevents the eels from escaping. Mr. Hiroshima learned this shape during his apprenticeship in 1930–32. Not only an important source of protein in the local diet, eels were also a source of income when taken live to market.

9 Basket for holding live eels
(unagi hogo)
Made by Hiroshima Kazuo, 1986
35 X 35 X 35

In contrast to the local shape (no. 8), this basket style was not used on the Gokase River. After Mr. Hiroshima moved to the riverside hamlet of Yato in 1959, he made one to order for a man from another region (he cannot recall precisely where), who had come to work at the electric power station in Yato. Thereafter, he filled six or seven orders from local people.

10 Creel

(biku)

Made by Hiroshima Kazuo, 1986

29 x 18 x 31

Fish caught in the Gokase River by rod and reel or trap (no. 19) were held in this type of creel. With the attached cord, a fisherman would tie the basket around his hips; the tight-fitting lid prevents the fish from leaping out. Mr. Hiroshima learned to make creels like this after moving to Gomi on the Gokase River in 1948.

11 Creel

(biku)

Made by Hiroshima Kazuo, 1986

31 x 22 x 35

Identical in function to no. 10, this creel is slightly larger and has an added band around the shoulder, to which the cord is attached.

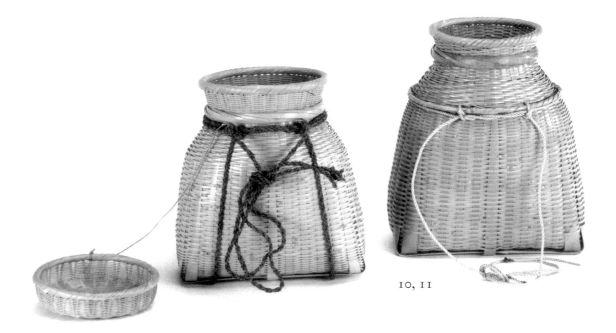

10, 11

12 Creel

(shitami)
Made by Hiroshima Kazuo, 1986
30 X 15 X 30

This type of creel was made to hold fish caught in the swift currents of mountain streams. During the high-water season, fishermen stood on the riverbank wielding large nets stretched within round bamboo frames at the end of six-meter-long bamboo poles *(tabusukui ami)*. They dropped their catch through the open stopper of the creel, which they tied around their hips with the attached cord; the ribs projecting from the lower edge of the stopper prevented the fish from jumping out. The creel could also be used for rod-and-reel fishing. Its body is densely woven while the angular shoulder is finished with a coarse weave to admit air.

Mr. Hiroshima learned to make this shape during his apprenticeship, but he modified it after 1948, when basketmaker Sasaki Hajime from Oita Prefecture showed him how to strengthen the basket by adding an extra ring around the neck *(kubiwa)* and reinforcing strips *(chikaradake)* on the sides.

12

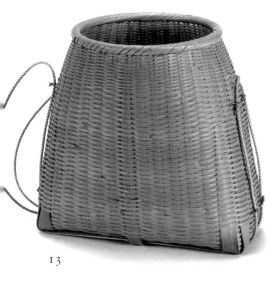

13

13 Basket for holding live sweetfish

(ayu kago)
Made by Hiroshima Kazuo, 1986
33 x 22 x 31

A basket like this was used on the lower reaches of the Gokase River specifically for keeping and transporting sweetfish *(ayu)*. After moving to Gomi in 1948, Mr. Hiroshima received orders for this type of basket from professional fishermen in Nobeoka, located at the mouth of the Gokase River.

14 Basket for holding live fish

(ikashi kago)
Made by Hiroshima Kazuo, 1986
65 x 65 x 39

Almost double the size of no. 8, this type of basket was also used for holding live eels or other fish; the close-fitting lid keeps eels from escaping. After moving to Yato in 1959, Mr. Hiroshima began making this shape to order for professional fishermen, who handled large quantities of eels. During the months of May and June, he would make two or three for brokers or restaurants specializing in river fish. He received orders for these baskets regularly until around 1965, after which demand dwindled, reflecting the lack of fish in the river as well as the replacement of bamboo baskets with plastic containers.

14

15 Basket for holding live fish
(ikashi kago)
Made by Hiroshima Kazuo, 1986
84 x 84 x 79

This type of basket was used from October through December to hold a day's catch of live sweetfish *(ayu)*. The fish traveled downriver to spawn and were caught in weirs set up by groups of fishermen at the rapids at Kawazuru and Okamoto. Around 1956, Mr. Hiroshima began taking orders from the groups and would make two or three such baskets each year. A basket would last four or five years, and each weir had six or seven baskets on hand. The bamboo strips for weaving *(higo)* were too long to be manipulated inside his Gomi workshop, so he assembled the baskets outdoors.

16

16 Basket for holding live fish
(ikashi kago)
Made by Hiroshima Kazuo, 1987
56 x 56 x 59
Smaller version of no. 15.

15

17 Trap for fish and river crabs

(saka uke or gani uke)
Made by Hiroshima Kazuo, 1986
38 x 38 x 61

The type of trap called *uke* is still used on the Gokase River between late August and October for catching river crabs, eels, and fish that come down-river to lay eggs. The trap consists of two cone-shaped baskets, one snug inside the other; the inside basket, which acts as a stopper, is open at both ends. The trap is placed horizontally in the water, with mouth facing upriver, and it is weighted with stones. Other stones are positioned to channel the flow of water through the trap so that the fish must swim into it. Long strips of bamboo at the inner edge of the removable stopper converge at the tips so that fish can swim in but not out; the stopper is tied in place with twine. This kind of basket may be made by an amateur.

18 Trap for rock trout

(aburame hibi)
Made by Hiroshima Kazuo, 1986
30 x 30 x 55

In small streams, this type of trap is baited with a mixture of rice bran and miso, which has been cooked to bring out the fragrance and then rolled into balls; the smell of the bait lures rock trout *(aburame)* into the trap. Like no. 17, the trap has a stopper that works as a one-way entrance. When Mr. Hiroshima apprenticed with Kudō Masanori in Kusubaru in 1930–32, his teacher fished with such a trap, but this practice was not widespread. Mr. Kudō made all his fishing equipment himself.

18, 17

19.1

19.1–2 Traps for dace

(ida hibi)

Made by Hiroshima Kazuo, 1986

51 x 51 x 51

Villagers on the Gokase River fill traps with fragrant bait (sweet-smelling sprouted barley or boiled ocean-fish bones) to catch the fish called dace (*ugui; ida* in local dialect). Dace live in one locale in the river; fishermen lower a trap into place to catch dace as they feed (the trap also catches carp, which have the same habits and like the same bait). The trap's rectangular mouth is fitted with a flexible gate made of bamboo strips, which prevents the fish from swim-ming out. The small dace are served as sashimi, large ones are broiled, then simmered in flavored sauce. Nowadays, with access to other fish, including frozen ocean fish, people eat dace less often.

A simple version of this kind of trap often was assembled by amateurs. In 1948, when Mr. Hiroshima moved to Gomi, he began receiving orders for such traps, and he improved upon the shape so that more fish could be caught: he flattened the base, increased the size of the opening through which fish entered, shifted the opening for removing the fish to the top of the basket, and widened that mouth and its stopper.

20, 21

20 Trap for river crabs

(gani hibi)
Made by Kai Akio, 1987
49 x 49 x 50

On dark nights between June and October, this sort of trap is tied down in sandy places of the Gokase River to lure river crabs, then it is pulled up and emptied in the morning. The crabs are attracted by the smell of bait (sardine bones and innards or chicken bones placed in an empty can). Kai Akio is a farmer in Takenohira hamlet in Hinokage who supplements his income by making bamboo baskets for his neighbors.

21 Trap for river crabs

(gani hibi)
Made by Hiroshima Kazuo, 1986
53 x 49 x 49

In constructing this trap, Mr. Hiroshima improved upon an amateur's basket (compare no. 20) by widening the entrance and adding a second opening for removing crabs. In the thirties and forties, fishing for abundant river crabs took place in October, about the time that corn ears ripened, and fishermen used the ears as bait.

22 Trap for carp

(koi hibi)
Made by Hiroshima Kazuo, 1987
87 x 82 x 69

Fishermen use traps like this on the lower reaches of the Gokase River to attract and catch carp *(koi)* through the scent of bait. Like dace, carp are bottom-feeders that live in one place in the river; this flat-bottomed trap is lowered onto the river bottom.

22

23 Trap for *enoha*

(enoha uke)
Made by Hiroshima Kazuo, 1986
35 x 35 x 79

This type of trap was designed to catch a pair of the slender, troutlike fish locally called *enoha* (*yamame* in standard Japanese) as they spawn. The changing color of the maple leaves used to be a reminder to put out traps in the small streams of the area. Mr. Hiroshima learned to make this simple basket as a boy in Mongyū. The trap is placed with its mouth facing upriver; the pair of mating fish is caught by the wide mouth and pushed by the current into the narrow, tubular end. Only one pair of fish can be caught at a time.

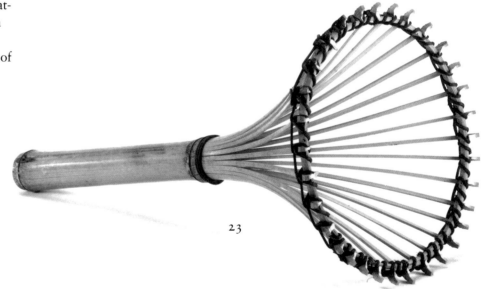

23

24.1–10 Traps for eels

(unagi poppo)
Made by Hiroshima Kazuo, 1987
7 x 7 x 59

Catching eels in traps like these was once a hobby for children. On the lower reaches of the Gokase River, eels are trapped as they swim upriver in May, June, and July. Baited with worms and weighted with stones on the sandy riverbed, the traps are positioned with the mouth facing downstream; they are put into place at night and emptied the next morning. The woven stopper with converging, sharp-pointed inner ends prevents the eels from escaping.

25.1–10 Small traps for eels

(unagi kappo)
Made by Hiroshima Kazuo, 1987
6 x 6 x 67

On the middle reaches of the Gokase River, fishermen usually used eel traps like these. Unlike the woven eel traps (no. 24), these are fashioned from lengths of bamboo; however, they are also fitted with woven stoppers.

26.1–3 Large traps for eels

(unagi kappo)
Made by Hiroshima Kazuo, 1987
9 x 9 x 95

Larger versions of no. 25; this size can hold five or six eels.

26.1, 25.1, 24.1

Kitchen and Farming Baskets

IN A HINOKAGE farmhouse that has not been remodeled, an old-fashioned kitchen is attached to one end of the building. This kitchen once served the needs of an extended family, which grew and processed most of its own food. In the center of the large room—with its pounded earth floor and high ceiling crossed by heavy wooden beams—stands a wood-burning stove made to hold massive iron kettles or stacked wooden steamers and other equipment for large-scale cooking and food processing. The kitchen door opens directly onto the farmyard; many tasks related to food preparation are performed outside on fine days.

A variety of baskets and tools made from bamboo were once abundant in Hinokage kitchens. One class of basket, made with an arched handle and a tight-fitting lid, served as a hanging pantry. In farming households twenty or thirty years ago, the women usually cooked hot rice for breakfast and again for the evening meal; they prepared extra rice in the morning to be set aside and eaten cold for the noonday meal. The rice was almost always mixed with barley or crushed corn kernels to make the rice harvest last the year. In the cool months, the cooked grain was kept in a bentwood container (no. 129); during the hot and humid summer, it was transferred to a rice-storage basket (nos. 1, 27, and 28) on top of a layer of cloth. To prevent cooked rice from spoiling, the basket was hung in the shade, usually under the deep eaves of the roof outside the kitchen. Farmers carried the basket to the field or mountainside and hung it from a tree branch out of reach of insects and animals. The lid's knob, made of a section of slender bamboo, was easy to grasp even with wet or muddy hands. Rice cakes *(mochi)* or leftovers were also kept in these baskets.

Suspended from the sooty beams of the kitchen, similar covered baskets (nos. 29–31) held sardines and other small fish, which households bought already processed. Caught in shallow coastal waters and then boiled and dried, these fish were sold by weight; the basket size was adjusted to hold a standard quantity. Women used dried fish to flavor the basic soup and stew broth *(dashi)*; the rehydrated fish were also made into a condiment rich in protein and calcium.

The single most widely used type of bamboo basket in Hinokage is the shallow, round-bottomed vessel with sturdy rim known locally as *shōke* (nos. 33–45). This is the basket that Mr. Hiroshima made in greatest quantity, in assorted sizes and variations, for farming households both before and after World War II. (Basketmakers were sometimes called by the pejorative term "*shōke* maker.") Even now, this colander-like vessel is effective for farming, commercial, and kitchen uses, especially for washing and draining grain and produce. The basketmaker weaves the *shōke* body with horizontal and vertical members in four-mesh plaiting (rather than in the "chrysanthemum" weave that radiates from the center); he binds the rim several times for strength.

27 Storage basket for cooked rice

(meshi kago)
Made by Hiroshima Kazuo, 1986
40 X 40 X 41

In the summer, cooked rice was stored in this type of basket, which was hung in a cool place. In the twenties and thirties, itinerant basketmakers made numerous rice-storage baskets; because it has a matching, snug-fitting lid, the basket is complicated to make and requires two full days to complete. Many households still use this basket type, since refrigeration hardens cooked rice.

28 Storage basket for cooked rice

(meshi kago)
Made by Hiroshima Kazuo, 1986
35 X 35 X 39

This basket serves the same function as no. 27, though it is made with a weave that Mr. Hiroshima learned from the Oita Prefecture basketmaker Sasaki Hajime. Mr. Sasaki specialized in winnows *(mi)* and other basketry using the *zarume* weave, in which fine horizontal strips are woven over wider vertical strips, starting with a "chrysanthemum" bottom. Colanders made with that weave are known as *zaru* instead of *shōke*.

29 Storage basket for dried sardines

(iriko kago)
Made by Hiroshima Kazuo, 1986
44 X 44 X 47

According to traditional Japanese measure, a lidded container of this size holds one *kan* of dried sardines (3.75 kilograms). Hung from the ceiling in the kitchen or storeroom, the basket could also be used for storing other foodstuffs. The three strips that make up the strong handle are secured with wild *tsuzura* vine.

Mr. Hiroshima learned this

27, 28

shape and that of the rice-storage basket (no. 27) during his apprenticeship in 1930–32 with Kudō Masanori; like the rice-storage basket, this lidded container takes two days to complete. The cost in 1932 was 1 yen 20 sen (100 sen equal 1 yen); by 1942, Mr. Hiroshima was charging 5 yen; in 1987, he charged 10,000 yen.

30 Storage basket for dried sardines

(iriko kago)
Made by Hiroshima Kazuo, 1986
34 x 34 x 41

Mr. Hiroshima invented this shape of storage basket in the fifties, when he was living in Gomi, by adding a handle to the eel basket he had learned to make during his apprenticeship (no. 8). The basket was popular and he received quite a few orders for it.

31 Storage basket for dried sardines

(iriko kago)
Made by Hiroshima Kazuo, 1986
31.5 x 31.5 x 40

This version of no. 30 stands on three legs made from sections of bamboo.

29, 30, 31

32, 33

32 Draining basket
for cups and bowls

(chawan kago)
Made by Hiroshima Kazuo, 1986
59 x 49 x 45

Containers of this shape are conve-
nient for draining and storing ceramic
rice bowls *(chawan)*, lacquered soup
bowls, chopsticks, and other table-
ware after they are washed. Before
farmhouses had running water, dishes
were washed in an outdoor trough or
in a nearby stream.

33 Storage basket

(sagejōke)
Made by Hiroshima Kazuo, 1986
53 x 55 x 42

This type of all-purpose basket is suspended in a cool place to store
steamed foods, such as wheat cakes
(dango), sweet potatoes, or ears of
corn, and keep them fresh. The shape
is the basic *shōke* with a strong handle composed of two bamboo strips.

34 Tray

(bara)

Made by Hiroshima Kazuo, 1986

74 x 74 x 9

The two-piece, hand-turned stone mill used for grinding grains into flour or beans into powder was placed on this type of tray, which is classified by function (rather than shape) as a type of *shōke*. The rim of the tray helped contain the flour, which could not leak through the tightly woven twill weave. Families infrequently mill at home today, but the basket is still handy for making glutinous-rice cakes *(mochi):* dusted with cornstarch, the tray is used as a surface for rolling out balls of rice that has been pounded into a paste in a foot-powered mill or wooden mortar.

34

35 Colander

(arajōke)
Made by Hiroshima Kazuo, 1987
69 x 69 x 14

This type of strong, versatile container serves many kitchen and farming functions. Using a colander this size or smaller, farming families collect and transport not only vegetables or grains harvested in the field but also fruits, nuts, or *shiitake* mushrooms gathered in the mountains. The coarsely woven center panel allows muddy produce or dirty dishes to be washed and drained in the container. After World War II, Mr. Hiroshima filled many orders for this size of colander to be used in the kitchens of Hinokage elementary schools.

36 Colander

(arajōke)
Made by Hiroshima Kazuo, 1986
64 x 64 x 12

Smaller version of no. 35.

37 Colander

(arajōke)
Made by Hiroshima Kazuo, 1987
50 x 50 x 10.5

Smaller version of no. 35.

35, 36, 37

38 Triangular colander

(sankakujōke)
Made by Hiroshima Kazuo, 1986
47 x 47 x 12

A triangular colander can be used for all the same tasks as a round colander (nos. 35–37); in addition, the narrow corners allow the basket to serve as a spouted *shōke* (no. 43) for transferring goods from one container to another. This versatile vessel was in steady demand until plastic substitutes became available.

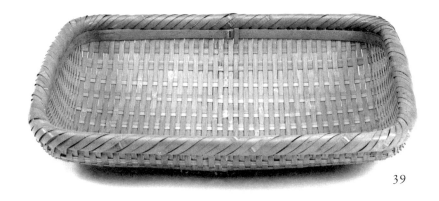

39

38

39 Rectangular colander

(shikakujōke)
Made by Hiroshima Kazuo, 1987
56 x 44 x 11.5

This rectangular version of nos. 35–37 seems to have been introduced to Hinokage from elsewhere, as Mr. Hiroshima does not recall making this shape during his apprenticeship. He would weave atypical colander and basket shapes whenever customers placed orders for them.

40 Fertilizer basket

(koejōke)
Made by Hiroshima Kazuo, 1986
51 x 51 x 9.5

In a carrying vessel like this, held level with both hands, farmers transported horse and cattle manure from the barn to the rice paddies or fields, where it was used as fertilizer.

41 Rice-rinsing colander

(komeagejōke)
Made by Hiroshima Kazuo, 1986
57 x 58 x 14

This type of tightly woven colander plays a role in the process of preparing cakes of pounded glutinous rice *(mochi):* the colander is used for draining the raw rice after it has soaked in water and transferring it into the steamer to be cooked. Hinokage households prepare *mochi* for festivals for the New Year, 3 March, and 5 May; for spring and autumn festivals at the village shrine; and for family celebrations. They also use this type of colander for preparing the vegetables used in the elaborate stews *(nishime)* served at festival gatherings. Because of its association with food preparation, the colander is stored carefully when not in use; many households have used the same basket for decades.

40

41, 42

42 Sake maker's rice-rinsing colander

(sakaya komeagejōke)
Made by Hiroshima Kazuo, 1986
66 x 67 x 16

The two sake breweries in Hinokage (Himeno Brewery and Fukuda Brewery) commissioned Mr. Hiroshima to make large colanders for washing and draining the rice used in preparing yeast as well as for carrying the fermented yeast. Rice grains do not cling to the smooth, finely woven surface.

43 Colander with pouring spout

(katakuchijōke or *inariguchi)*
Made by Hiroshima Kazuo, 1986
47 x 51 x 12

The open spout on this basket type makes it useful for transferring drained rice into the steamer when it is used instead of the rice-rinsing colander (no. 41). The basket is also handy for transferring grains or beans into storage containers without spilling them, and it can be used as an ordinary colander.

44 Parboiled-barley colander with pouring spout

(mugiyomashijōke)
Made by Hiroshima Kazuo, 1986
48 x 49 x 11

Except on special occasions, farming families rarely ate unmixed rice for their meals; they usually combined it with another grain, most typically barley. Since whole-grain barley takes longer to cook than rice, it was boiled separately and drained in a colander like this before being added to the pot as the rice came to a boil. Once machines were developed to process flattened barley, which cooks quickly, this procedure became unnecessary. Mr. Hiroshima first made this specialized shape after World War II when he was living in Unama hamlet in Kitagō Village; the shape was not used in Hinokage.

43, 44

45

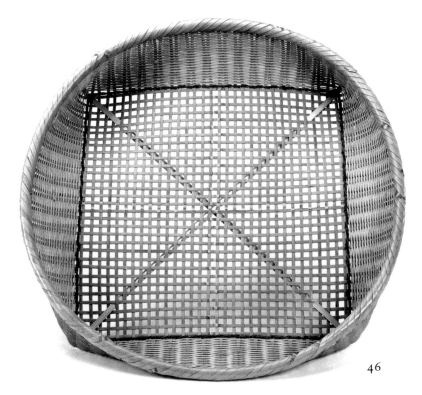

46

45 Taro-washing colander
(imoaraijōke)
Made by Hiroshima Kazuo, 1987
54.5 X 55 X 13

A colander like this was employed in the process of preparing taro *(imo):* the tubers were first stirred with a wooden pole in a wooden bucket of water to remove their thin, muddy skins, then turned out into this type of basket to be rinsed with fresh water and drained.

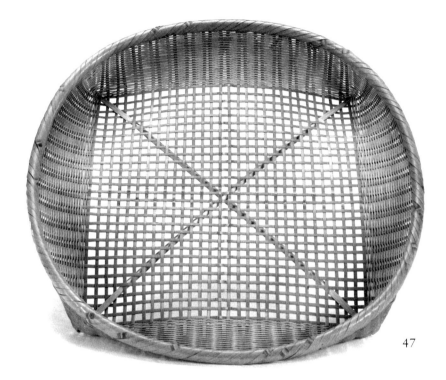

47

It has a precisely spaced open weave in the center panel. The size of the mesh is expressed in the traditional measurement of *bu* (3.03 millimeters). All such sieving baskets are painstaking to produce and require special tools (nos. 154 and 156).

47 Chaff sieve

(momi tōshi), 2.5-*bu* mesh
Made by Hiroshima Kazuo, 1986
65.5 x 65.5 x 10

This chaff sieve is a wider-mesh version of no. 46. Although the size of the mesh determines the size of grain to be sorted, most households seem to have made do with a single sieve for all purposes. Since the sieve was a specialized and costly tool, each farmhouse would commission only one and would use it carefully; Mr. Hiroshima did not receive as many orders for sieves as for colanders.

46 Chaff sieve

(momi tōshi), 2-*bu* mesh
Made by Hiroshima Kazuo, 1986
63 x 63 x 11

A chaff sieve was used for separating husked rice grains *(momi)* from husks and debris or for cleaning other grains and beans (such as wheat, barley, millet, *azuki* beans, and soybeans) of their husks or dried pods. After being sorted with this sieve, the grain was further processed using a winnow. Mr. Hiroshima learned to make this implement during his apprenticeship.

48 Tea sieve

(cha tōshi), 1.5-*bu* mesh
Made by Hiroshima Kazuo, 1986
49 x 49 x 9.5

In the style of tea processing common in Hinokage farming households, the leaves are first parched in a flat iron kettle then kneaded into cylindrical rolls. In the final step, a tea sieve is used to grade the leaves by size (the desirable fine leaves fall through) and also sort out debris such as twigs. Mr. Hiroshima's teacher Kudō Masanori taught him how to construct this implement, which takes an entire day to make. Since pan-roasted tea is still a major product of Hinokage, almost every household uses and preserves a tea sieve ordered long ago.

49 Tea sieve

(cha tōshi), 2-*bu* mesh
Made by Hiroshima Kazuo, 1986
48.5 x 49 x 10

Wider-mesh version of no. 48.

50 Sieve for crushed corn kernels

(kozane tōshi)
Made by Hiroshima Kazuo, 1986
57.5 x 57 x 7

In Hinokage, rice was often cooked together with crushed kernels of corn *(tōkibi)*. The kernels were ground in a hand-turned stone mill to produce particles of the same size as rice grains, so that they would cook in the same amount of time. A sieve like this was used for sizing the particles and removing debris. Since its use was so specialized, it did not wear out; old examples survive in many households (see no. 2).

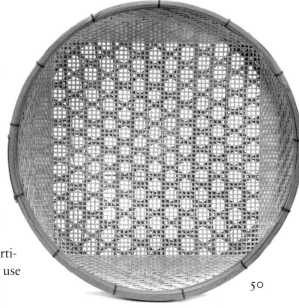

50

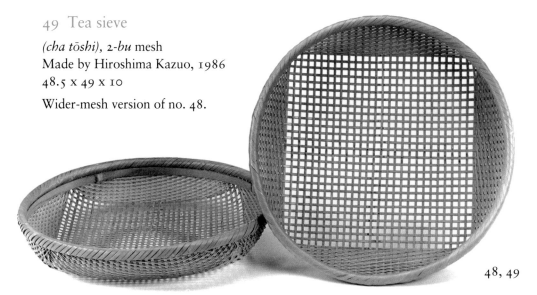

48, 49

51.1–2 Bean-paste sieves

(miso koshi)
Made by Hiroshima Kazuo, 1986
25 x 25 x 10

A bean-paste sieve was essential for making *miso shiru* soup. In the past, almost all Hinokage households produced their own fermented soybean paste (miso). Homemade miso retains the shapes of the soybeans and barley used as ingredients. To make soup, an appropriate quantity of miso is placed in the sieve, which is immersed in the kettle of boiling water while the miso is stirred with chopsticks or a ladle until it dissolves. The bean-paste sieve was made to fit the family's kettle, which in turn reflected the number of people in the household. This simple basket shape is the first form that Mr. Hiroshima learned as an apprentice basketmaker.

52 Bean-paste sieve with handle

(tetsuki miso koshi)
Made by Hiroshima Kazuo, 1987
68 x 26 x 15

This utensil performs the same function as no. 51. The length of bamboo that serves as the handle is split at one end to form the ribs of the sieve.

53 Noodle scoop

(udon age)
Made by Hiroshima Kazuo, 1987
71 x 26 x 5

A noodle scoop is used to retrieve *udon* (thick wheat-flour noodles) or *soba* (buckwheat noodles) out of the large kettle of boiling water in which they are cooked. It can also be used for removing cooked dumplings *(dango)* or cakes of devil's tongue jelly *(konnyaku)* from boiling water.

52, 51.1, 53

54

54 Soy-sauce filter

(su)

Made by Hiroshima Kazuo, 1987

23 x 23 x 76

For the process of making soy sauce *(shoyu)* at home, a filter is embedded in the center of a flat-bottomed wooden barrel containing a thick mixture of cooked soybeans, barley, yeast, salt, and water *(moromi)*. The liquid from this mixture, which is soy sauce, seeps into the cylinder and can be drawn off with a ladle; the filter also strains off any impurities in the *moromi*. Water is added to the *moromi* to make two additional decoctions of soy sauce.

55.1–2 Salt-draining baskets

(shio kago)

Made by Hiroshima Kazuo, 1987

24 x 24.5 x 45

In the past, salt was a precious commodity in mountain communities because it was not available locally and had to be purchased in bulk out of large wooden buckets. Unrefined sea salt—the form that was sold in the past—retained a certain amount of moisture; when it was stored in this type of hanging basket, the moisture drained off or "wept" through the pointed tip into a bowl below. The draining process prevented the salt from caking, and the liquid, called bittern, or *nigari*, was used as the solidifier for making homemade soybean curd (tofu). Even today, many Hinokage women make tofu for their own household's use.

55.1

56 Drainer

(tarashi)
Made by Hiroshima Kazuo, 1987
38 x 29.5 x 5

Flat rectangular containers with open-weave bases were used in urban kitchens for draining washed vegetables. The shape did not originate in Hinokage, where villagers used the large, round-bottomed colander. Mr. Hiroshima learned this shape during World War II, when he worked at the Satō Shin'ichi workshop in Nobeoka. While in Nobeoka, Mr. Hiroshima added many unfamiliar basket shapes to his repertory, but he has forgotten most of them.

57 Drainer

(tarashi)
Made by Hiroshima Kazuo, 1987
34 x 27.5 x 5

Smaller version of no. 56.

58 Drainer

(tarashi)
Made by Hiroshima Kazuo, 1987
32 x 25.5 x 4.5

Smaller version of no. 56.

56, 57, 58

59 Hip basket

(tego)

Made by Hiroshima Kazuo, 1986

33 x 26 x 34

Tied around the hips with a cord, this type of basket leaves both hands free for picking tea leaves, *shiitake,* or fruit. A hip basket is also used to carry rice seed to be broadcast in the seedbed or to hold rice seedlings to be transplanted into the flooded paddy field. Various shapes of *tego* were once in common use, but this was the shape that Mr. Hiroshima made most often for the important Hinokage crops of *shiitake* and tea. (Such baskets are sometimes designated by use as *nabatori tego* for *shiitake* or *chatori tego* for tea.)

60 Open-weave hip basket

(me tego)

Made by Hiroshima Kazuo, 1986

33.5 x 22 x 31

The open weave *(me)* of this version of no. 59 allows water to drain out, so it is particularly suitable for holding rice seedlings for transplanting or weeds pulled in the paddy field.

61 Hip basket in shape of backpack basket

(karuigata tego)

Made by Hiroshima Kazuo, 1986

35 x 22.5 x 30

This basket shape serves the same functions as the standard hip basket (no. 59), but it is fashioned in the form of the backpack called *karui,* which is distinctive to the Hinokage region. Many Hinokage farmers are capable of making *karui,* so this type of *tego* is common. The technique follows that of the *karui* with three horizontal bands (nos. 94, 96, and 97).

59, 60, 61

62 *Shiitake* sieve

(naba tōshi), 7-*bu* mesh
Made by Hiroshima Kazuo, 1986
75 x 74 x 12

Local people who specialize in raising and drying *shiitake* use sieves to grade the mushrooms into standard sizes; pre-sorting allows them to sell the mushrooms for a better price to the wholesaler. This type of sieve grades *shiitake* with diameters of 7 *bu* (2.11 centimeters). Mr. Hiroshima also supplied sieves to *shiitake* wholesalers. From local farmers, he received numerous orders for sets consisting of this type of sieve and the twill-weave winnow (no. 69). Production of a *shiitake* sieve is painstaking because the mesh has to be uniform, and the weaving strips *(higo)* are liable to break at the right-angle corners between the base and rim.

62

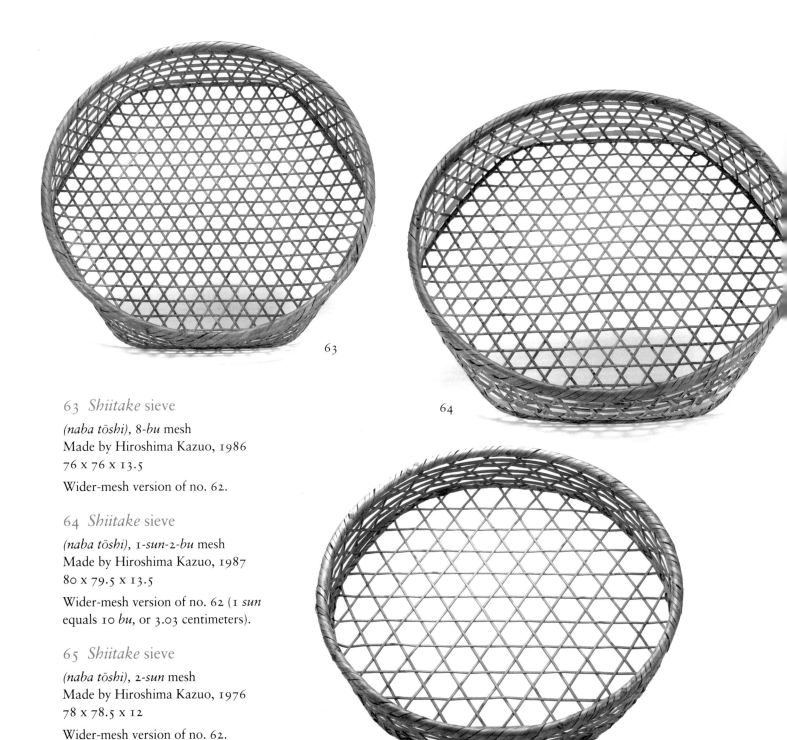

63

63 *Shiitake* sieve

(naba tōshi), 8-*bu* mesh
Made by Hiroshima Kazuo, 1986
76 x 76 x 13.5

Wider-mesh version of no. 62.

64 *Shiitake* sieve

(naba tōshi), 1-*sun*-2-*bu* mesh
Made by Hiroshima Kazuo, 1987
80 x 79.5 x 13.5

Wider-mesh version of no. 62 (1 *sun*
equals 10 *bu*, or 3.03 centimeters).

65 *Shiitake* sieve

(naba tōshi), 2-*sun* mesh
Made by Hiroshima Kazuo, 1976
78 x 78.5 x 12

Wider-mesh version of no. 62.

64

65

66 Charcoal sieve

(ebu or *sumi tōshi),* 3-*bu* mesh
Made by Hiroshima Kazuo, 1987
58 x 60 x 25

Charcoal makers sieve sticks of charcoal that have been prepared in the kiln, to separate the ash before the charcoal is packed into bales (*tawara,* usually wrapped in woven rice-straw mats). The ash is used by other tradespeople like blacksmiths and dyers. For some time after the end of World War II, charcoal was the major heating fuel in Japan; consequently, charcoal production flourished in mountainous regions, such as the remote hamlet of Mongyū where Mr. Hiroshima grew up. Charcoal makers usually constructed their own sieves; however, Mr. Hiroshima received orders from time to time.

67 Charcoal sieve

(ebu or *sumi tōshi),* 5-*bu* mesh
Made by Hiroshima Kazuo, 1987
57.5 x 62 x 26

Wider-mesh version of no. 66.

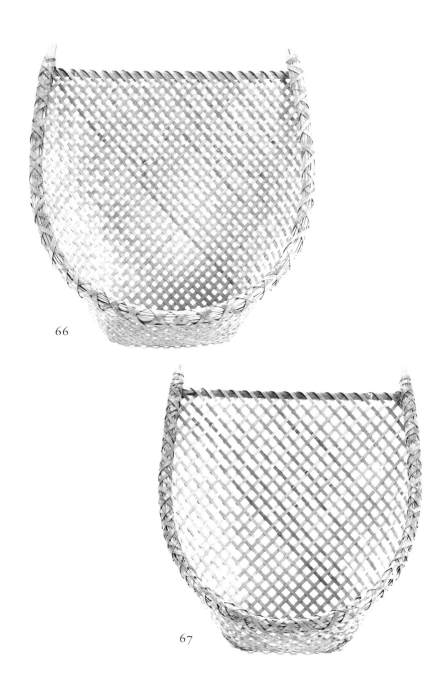

66

67

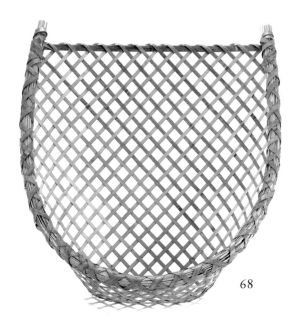

68 Charcoal sieve

(ebu or *sumi tōshi), 7-bu* mesh
Made by Hiroshima Kazuo, 1987
59 x 62 x 28

Wider-mesh version of no. 66. This size of sieve was used to scoop up the finished charcoal from the kiln and transfer it into bales.

68

69 Twill-weave winnow

(ajiro mi)
Made by Hiroshima Kazuo, 1986
66 x 63.5 x 22

This type of winnow, woven in twill weave, is used to sift the debris from dried *shiitake* and to transfer the mushrooms into bags or boxes. Mr. Hiroshima made these types of baskets for the local *shiitake* wholesalers (Kawasaki Store, Sugimoto Store) and for farmhouses specializing in large-scale *shiitake* production. The winnow was used in a set with the *shiitake* sieve (nos. 62–65).

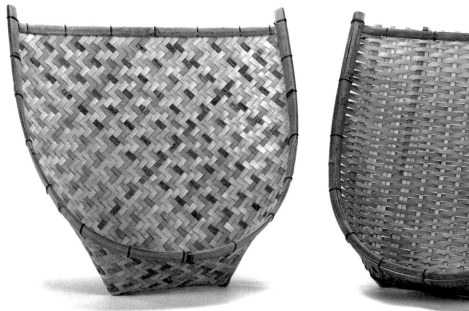

69, 70

70 Fodder colander

(hamikuwasejōke)
Made by Hiroshima Kazuo, 1987
64 x 63 x 22

This type of flat-bottomed scoop is used to prepare finely chopped dried grass and leaves *(hami)* as fodder for cattle and horses during the winter and to transfer it into the wooden feeding trough. In Hinokage, where many households keep cattle, this is a common basket type.

71

71 Hemp-thread container

(ogoke)
Made by Hiroshima Kazuo, 1986
31 x 31 x 23.5

This type of container was required in the process of preparing thread from the bast fiber of hemp, known as *taima* in Japanese. Women stripped the fibers from the retted stalks and knotted them end to end to make a continuous thread that was coiled into this container for safe storage. Until recently, hemp and related fibers were a major source of the textiles woven and used in rural households, especially in mountainous areas, for garments, bedding, and storage bags. Cotton could not be grown in the mountains, and homespun cotton could not withstand the rough usage given to work garments. Although basketmakers often made this type of basket in the late nineteenth and early twentieth century, Mr. Hiroshima received almost no orders for the product, because heavy mill-woven cloth and commercial work clothes had eliminated the need for hemp cloth.

72 Delivery basket

(jitensha kago)
Made by Hiroshima Kazuo, 1986
56 x 41 x 34

Strapped to the carrying rack of a bicycle or motorcycle, this sturdy basket type was used by local shops to make deliveries. Orders came mainly from people who lived along paved roads, although Mr. Hiroshima also received some requests from farming families who owned bicycles. After World War II, once most Hinokage roads were paved and bicycles became common, Mr. Hiroshima made many of these baskets for the two local sake breweries. This version was sized to hold twelve large bottles (1 *shō* or 1.8 liters) of sake or barley liquor *(shōchū)*. Mr. Hiroshima tried to weave this shape by copying examples until Mr. Tanaka and Mr. Okita, two Nobeoka basketmakers he met in the Satō Shin'ichi workshop during the war, taught him the necessary tricks concerning the measurements of weaving strips for the bottom and sides of the basket and preparation of the reinforcing strips for the corners and rim.

73 Delivery basket

(jitensha kago)
Made by Hiroshima Kazuo, 1987
48 x 36 x 30

Smaller version of no. 72, a basket this size can hold eight 1-*shō* bottles of sake.

74 Delivery basket

(jitensha kago)
Made by Hiroshima Kazuo, 1987
43 x 29.5 x 28

Smaller version of no. 72, a basket this size can hold six 1-*shō* bottles of sake.

72, 73, 74

75 Tea-leaf basket

(namaha kago)
Made by Hiroshima Kazuo, 1987
86 x 64 x 17

This large, shallow basket shape is used primarily in tea-processing plants to collect and cool the roasted tea leaves.

76 Tea-leaf basket

(cha kago)
Made by Hiroshima Kazuo, 1986
64.5 x 64 x 69

In tea-processing plants, the tea leaves picked in the months of April and May are stored in baskets like this until they are processed. Mr. Hiroshima also supplied large tea-leaf baskets to Hinokage households that had large numbers of tea bushes.

77 Tea-leaf basket

(cha kago)
Made by Hiroshima Kazuo, 1987
42 x 41.5 x 41

Tea leaves harvested into hip baskets (no. 59) were emptied into a basket this size to be delivered to the processing plant.

77, 75, 76

78 Mulberry-leaf basket

(kuwa kago)
Made by Hiroshima Kazuo, 1987
61 x 61 x 66

Silkworm-raising was an occupation in some Hinokage farm households through the twenties and thirties. The process requires large quantities daily of fresh mulberry leaves to satisfy the worms' voracious appetite. The leaves were harvested into hip baskets, which were emptied into baskets of this shape and kept in the room where the worms were being raised.

79 Mulberry-leaf basket

(kuwa kago)
Made by Hiroshima Kazuo, 1987
56 x 56.5 x 65

Smaller version of no. 78.

79, 78

80–81 Tray and stand for drying *shiitake*

(ama and *amadai)*
Made by Hiroshima Kazuo, 1987
103 x 103 x 20; 97.5 x 96 x 50.5

This type of dome-shaped tray and its tall cylindrical stand are used for drying fresh *shiitake* over a charcoal fire lit inside the stand. As a lightweight, portable stove, this set of baskets is a flexible alternative to drying the mushrooms over the wood-burning kitchen stove (see no. 83). The dome shape of the tray keeps the mushrooms on top farthest away from the hottest part of the coals, to avoid being scorched. Oil-burning stoves have recently replaced this basket set, which was once found in almost every Hinokage household. *Shiitake* cultivation is a profitable source of income in Hinokage; Mr. Hiroshima remembers that he started making *ama* as soon as he began his apprenticeship.

80, 81

82 Tea-kneading tray

(cha momi)
Made by Hiroshima Kazuo, 1987
97.5 x 63.5 x 3.5

In the *kamairi* method of processing tea, which is practiced in Hinokage, the leaves are parched in a dry iron kettle then kneaded by hand on this flat tray and formed into rolls. In the absence of a tray like this, a woven mat can be used.

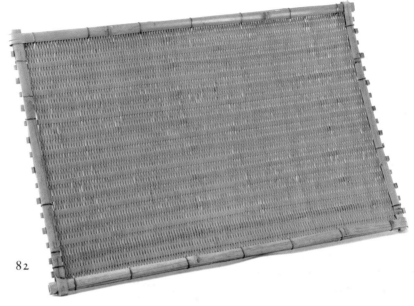

82

83 *Shiitake* dryer

(naba aburi)
Made by Hiroshima Kazuo, 1987
84 x 84 x 6

In this version of equipment for drying fresh *shiitake* (compare nos. 80–81), the basket is placed over the wide round opening of a traditional wood-burning kitchen stove, and the heat of the fire dries the mushrooms. This process is easy to use for a small *shiitake* harvest.

83

84 Openwork tray for raising silkworms

(kaiko bara)
Made by Hiroshima Kazuo, 1987
90 x 60 x 4

Silkworms graze on fresh mulberry leaves, which are spread out on this type of wood-framed structure. It is used as a set with a second, solidly woven basket that collects the feces from the worms (no. 85). Many such sets were needed to raise silkworms; they were placed on racks in a room in the house dedicated to this purpose. Raising silkworms was an active industry in Hinokage from the mid-nineteenth to the early twentieth century; up to about 1936, Mr. Hiroshima supplied improved versions of openwork trays to four or five Hinokage households that continued the work. Since raising silkworms required so many baskets, which would be expensive to commission, they were usually made by the men of the household.

85 Solid-weave tray for raising silkworms

(kaiko bara)
90 x 60 x 42
Made by Hiroshima Kazuo, 1987

Placed under the openwork tray on which the silkworms feed (no. 84), this type of twill-woven tray collects the feces.

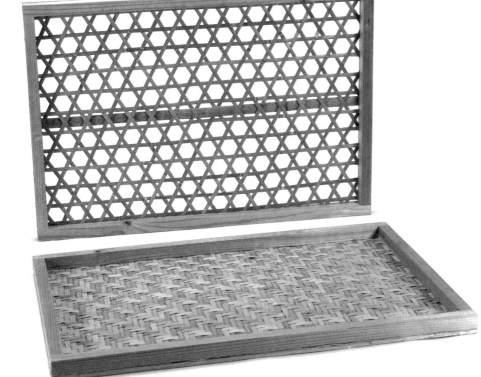

84, 85

86

86 Funnel

(jōgo)
Made by Hiroshima Kazuo, 1986
47 x 47 x 36

A large-capacity funnel was used for filling straw bags with dried grains and beans. Mr. Hiroshima recalls that basketmakers commonly made bamboo funnels until about 1925, when galvanized steel funnels became widely available; the only basketmaker who continued to weave funnels was Ushi-don (Hiraoka Ushimatsu).

87 Chick cage

(hiyoko kago)
Made by Hiroshima Kazuo, 1987
81 x 82 x 52

With a large, open-weave cover like this, farmers kept predators (such as the house cat or wild dogs) away from the chicks in the farmyard.

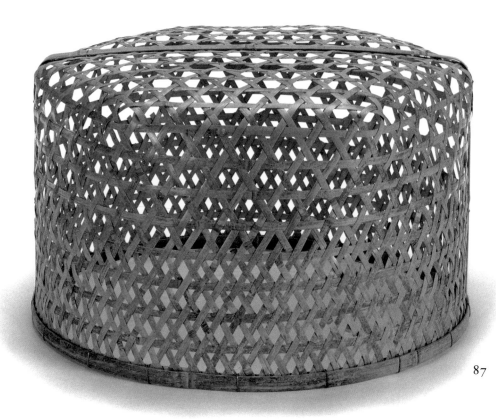

87

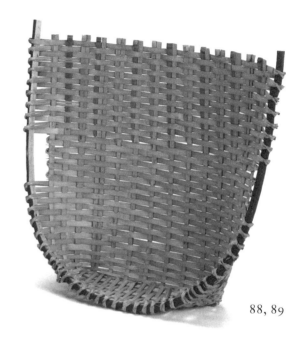

88, 89

88 Carrying fan

(te mi)
Made by Hiroshima Kazuo, 1987
42 x 42 x 10

Made to be gripped firmly with two hands, carrying fans were used when preparing new paddy fields or doing other construction that involved moving clods of earth, sand, or gravel. This sturdy basket is made with thick strips of bamboo and a heavily reinforced rim. Mr. Hiroshima constructed many such baskets during World War II while working at the Satō Shin'ichi workshop in Nobeoka; demand for them from Hinokage construction companies continued until the early sixties. About ten carrying fans could be made in a day.

89 Earth-carrying basket

(tsuchi kakae)
Made by Hiroshima Kazuo, 1987
52 x 48 x 18

This type of basket, similar to no. 88, was used especially for moving earth clods in the process of converting a field into a rice paddy.

90 Stretcher

(mokko)
Made by Hiroshima Kazuo, 1987
181 x 63 x 4

When preparing a new rice paddy,
teams of two people used a stretcher
to carry away heavy loads of earth. It
could also be used for transporting
manure to be used as fertilizer.
Children carried away leaves and
other debris on a stretcher when
cleaning the schoolyard.

90

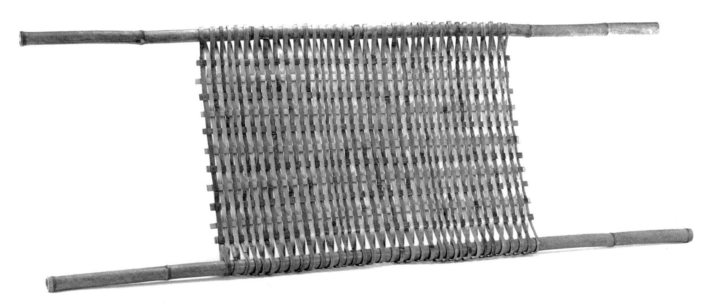

91

91 Shoulder-pole balance baskets

(kansuke kago)
Made by Hiroshima Kazuo, 1987
176 x 56 x 19

In the lowland area around Unama hamlet in Kitagō Village, over the mountain from Hinokage, farmers balanced a pair of baskets on a shoulder pole to transport loads or carry seedlings to the rice paddies. That method was not practical in mountainous Hinokage. Mr. Hiroshima learned to make the balance baskets, as well as the local styles of backpack basket (nos. 104–6), during the two years just after World War II when he lived in his older sister's home in Unama.

Backpack Baskets

A BASKET woven in a reverse triangular shape, the *karui* is peculiar to the Hinokage and adjacent Takachiho and Gokase regions in Miyazaki Prefecture and the Aso region of Oita Prefecture. In this basket, the weaving strips *(higo)* are bent in the middle to form the base. Then they are woven vertically around horizontal bands, called *obi* or *wa*, whose number (three, five, or seven) is the basis for designating the type of *karui*. A three-*wa karui* is light and open; a seven-*wa karui* is closely woven. The five-*wa karui* is least common. The overall shape is an inverted triangle, with narrow base and wide top. This is the most suitable shape for carrying loads on steep mountain slopes; even very heavy loads can be carried without strain.

The various *karui* shapes fulfill all types of transportation functions, and every farmhouse stocks a large assortment. Farmers use the *karui* in the fields, to carry tools or transport harvested crops; for work in the mountains, to transport tools and a packed lunch; when going to the market in town, to transport goods to be sold and purchased. Mr. Hiroshima used to carry his basketmaking tools in a *karui* when he was making the rounds of the farming hamlets.

Thirty years ago, most men in farming households were able to weave *karui* baskets. Professional basketmakers who began producing *karui* standardized the shapes and sizes. However, a great variety of sturdy shapes made by amateurs can still be seen, and there are many people around who can construct their own baskets. The fact that the basket is in widespread use today indicates how well-suited it is to local working and living conditions.

92, 93

92 Five-band backpack basket

(itsusuwagarui)
Made by Hiroshima Kazuo, 1987
47 x 38 x 41

In this *karui* basket, Mr. Hiroshima wove the body with five horizontal bands, creating a lighter version than the standard, more densely woven seven-band backpack (nos. 93 and 98–103).

93 Seven-band backpack basket

(nanatsuwagarui)
Made by Hiroshima Kazuo, 1987
57 x 47 x 48

With a body woven over seven horizontal bands, this deeper version of the *karui* backpack basket is less liable to spill its contents when the wearer is moving over steep terrain. The seven-band *karui* is the most common *karui* configuration.

94

94 Fertilizer backpack basket

(koe karui)
Made by Hiroshima Kazuo, 1987
63 x 51 x 53

This particular type of *karui*, constructed with three horizontal bands and wide vertical strips in a coarse, open weave, is used to carry cow manure from the barn to the fields for use as fertilizer.

95 Gravel backpack basket

(barasugarui)
Made by Iiboshi Itsuo, 1987
56 x 44 x 44

This and the next eight baskets are the work of Hinokage farmer Iiboshi Itsuo (born 1928), who specializes in weaving *karui* of many sizes and varieties. He learned to make *karui* from watching his father, a carpenter, make them in his spare time. It takes Mr. Iiboshi a day to complete one *karui*, and he makes about three hundred in a year.

This type of *karui* is meant for transporting gravel or crushed rock for construction projects. Since even a small load of such materials is quite heavy, the *karui* is small and solidly constructed with three horizontal bands and wide vertical strips for sturdiness.

96 Fertilizer backpack basket

(koe karui)
Made by Iiboshi Itsuo, 1987
67 x 56 x 52

This basket has the same function as no. 94 made by Hiroshima Kazuo but shows the slight differences in another basketmaker's work.

97 Double-load backpack basket

(nikairigarui)
Made by Iiboshi Itsuo, 1987
88 x 65 x 65

This capacious type of *karui* carries
an outsized "double load" of bulky
but lightweight materials, such as
dried grass, rice straw, or dried leaves.
It is twice the size of the standard
three-band *karui*.

95, 96, 97

98–103

98 Seven-band backpack basket

(nanatsuwagarui)
Made by Iiboshi Itsuo, 1987
41 x 38 x 34

Mr. Iiboshi's version of no. 93.

99 Seven-band backpack basket

(nanatsuwagarui)
Made by Iiboshi Itsuo, 1987
48 x 40 x 38

Larger version of no. 98.

100 Seven-band backpack basket

(nanatsuwagarui)
Made by Iiboshi Itsuo, 1987
51 x 45 x 43

Larger version of no. 98.

101 Seven-band backpack basket

(nanatsuwagarui)
Made by Iiboshi Itsuo, 1987
57 x 48 x 47

Larger version of no. 98.

102 Seven-band backpack basket

(nanatsuwagarui)
Made by Iiboshi Itsuo, 1987
62 x 49 x 51

Larger version of no. 98.

103 Seven-band backpack basket

(nanatsuwagarui)
Made by Iiboshi Itsuo, 1987
67 x 53 x 58

Larger version of no. 98.

104 Backpack basket for harvesting *shiitake*

(nabatori hogo)
Made by Hiroshima Kazuo, 1986
54 X 43 X 65

This type of backpack was used in Unama hamlet of adjacent Kitagō Village chiefly for gathering and transporting fresh *shiitake* but also for harvesting buckwheat, millet, and Deccan grass or for collecting fertilizer. The basket was a basic tool of the farming households in the gently rolling region, but its broad base and resultant low center of gravity made it unsuitable for the steep paths of Hinokage. The weaving technique differs from that of the *karui*.

105 Backpack basket for harvesting *shiitake*

(nabatori hogo)
Made by Hiroshima Kazuo, 1986
71 X 45 X 79

A larger version of no. 104, modified by the addition of a conical collar, this type of basket was also used in Unama hamlet of Kitagō Village. The collar probably represents an unknown basketmaker's improvement on the basic basket to enlarge its capacity.

104, 105

106

106 Unama backpack basket

(Unama kago)
Made by Hiroshima Kazuo, 1986
38 x 26 x 42

Unama hamlet in Kitagō Village gave its name to this tightly woven backpack basket, which is widely used for various shopping and transporting purposes. The shape is not known in adjacent Hinokage. With its fine weave, the basket can hold loose grains. During the war Unama baskets were used to carry rationed rice from the distribution center.

107 Nanatsuyama backpack basket

(Nanatsuyamagarui)
Made by Hiroshima Kazuo, 1987
48 x 43 x 47

This backpack basket is another village's version of a backpack basket for use in mountainous terrain. Peculiar to Nanatsuyama hamlet of adjoining Morotsuka Village, the basket is roughly woven with the narrow base and wide opening suited for use on steep slopes.

107

Objects Made from Lengths of Bamboo Stalks

A BASKETMAKER prepares his weaving strips by trimming the bamboo and then slicing it repeatedly until it yields a set of uniformly thin strips; however, he also uses whole sections of bamboo stalk to fashion some essential tools and vessels. A strong membrane spans each node of a bamboo stalk, so the entire stalk comprises many enclosed segments. Mr. Hiroshima constructed the tools and vessels catalogued here more as illustrations of the extensive use of bamboo than as examples of a professional basketmaker's skill.

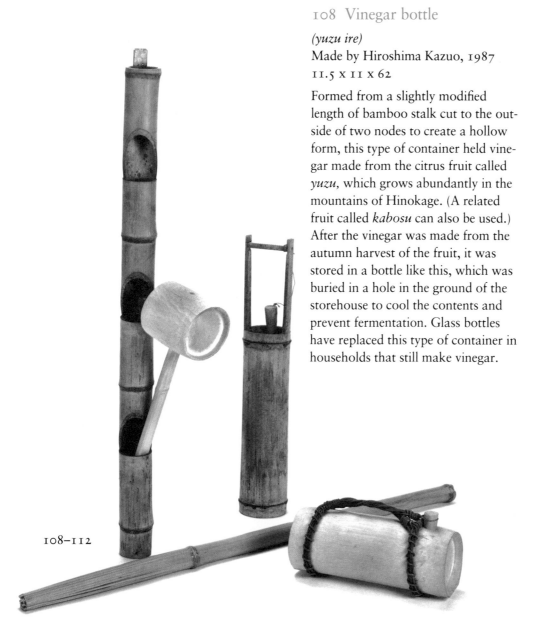

108–112

108 Vinegar bottle

(yuzu ire)
Made by Hiroshima Kazuo, 1987
11.5 x 11 x 62

Formed from a slightly modified length of bamboo stalk cut to the outside of two nodes to create a hollow form, this type of container held vinegar made from the citrus fruit called *yuzu,* which grows abundantly in the mountains of Hinokage. (A related fruit called *kabosu* can also be used.) After the vinegar was made from the autumn harvest of the fruit, it was stored in a bottle like this, which was buried in a hole in the ground of the storehouse to cool the contents and prevent fermentation. Glass bottles have replaced this type of container in households that still make vinegar.

109 Canteen

(yogiri poppo)
Made by Hiroshima Kazuo, 1987
33.5 x 16 x 17

Made from a length of stalk cut to the outside of two nodes so as to form a natural container, a canteen like this would have held drinking water (or alcohol) for taking to work in the mountains or for traveling. The variety of bamboo usually used for this vessel was the large-stemmed, heavy *mōsō (Phyllostachys pubescens).*

110 Ladle

(hishaku)
Made by Hiroshima Kazuo, 1987
48 x 12 x 17

Cut from a section of bamboo, with the node forming the base, this type of ladle was used for dipping water out of a large storage vat or soy sauce from a filter like no. 54.

111 Kitchen utensil holder

(fuyuji)
Made by Hiroshima Kazuo, 1987
7 x 7 x 103

Fashioned from a multinoded length of bamboo with one opening cut above each node, a receptacle like this hangs on the kitchen wall to store chopsticks, rice scoops, noodle scoops (no. 53), ladles (no. 110), and other utensils within easy reach.

113

112 Bean-curd stirrer

(tofu maze)
Made by Hiroshima Kazuo, 1987
4.2 x 4.2 x 116

A simple length of bamboo is used to stir the kettle of simmering soybeans, the main ingredient of tofu. Bamboo is a practical material for stirrers because it does not become hot when immersed in the pot.

113 Shelf

(sana)
Made by Hiroshima Kazuo, 1987
72 x 25 x 5

A portable shelf, constructed from several lengths of bamboo split in half lengthwise and bound with cord, has various uses. For example, placed across the rim of a wooden bucket, it supports the stone mill used to grind soybeans in the process of making tofu. It is also used to drain the solidified bean curd.

114 Canteen for bait fish

(yogiri or *otori ire)*
Maker and date unknown
Gift of Ōsaka Chiaki, Nishi Hinokage
36 x 10 x 10

From May through August, fishermen sometimes caught sweetfish *(ayu)* by using a small *ayu,* with hooks attached to its tail and a fishing line through its nose, as bait. Highly territorial, a sweetfish attacks any competitor that enters its domain: a sweetfish attacking the bait *(otori)* would get caught on the hooks. The bait fish was kept in a canteen like this.

114

Toys

AS A TREAT for the children of the household for which he was working, Mr. Hiroshima would make a few toys. He did not charge for the playthings, which were also a form of rest and amusement for the craftsman tired of making baskets. The simple toys could also be made by the children or their parents; in fact, Mr. Nakamura as a child played with stilts and water guns that he made himself.

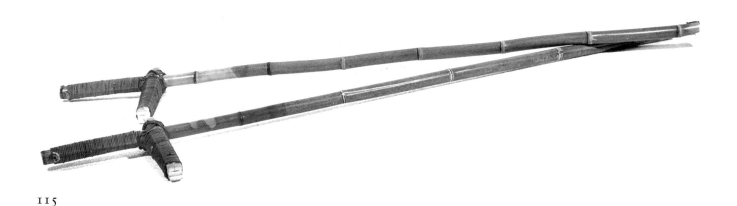

115

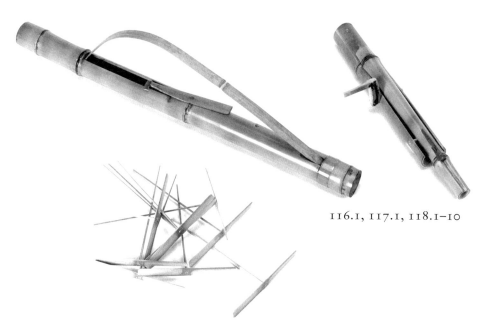

116.1, 117.1, 118.1–10

117.1–3 Toy antiaircraft guns

(kikanjū)
Made by Hiroshima Kazuo, 1987
38 x 11 x 6

When Mr. Hiroshima was working as an itinerant craftsman, local children would gather around to watch him spread out his tools in a farmyard, and he would make this kind of toy antiaircraft gun for them. The Japanese campaign against China had begun in 1935 and war games were extremely popular among children. To the children's delight, the guns were constructed so that they could shoot stones.

115 Stilts

(take uma)
Made by Hiroshima Kazuo, 1987
29 x 13 x 177

Children used to play with stilts made from lengths of bamboo fitted with footrests.

116.1–5 Toy guns

(hajiki teppo)
Made by Hiroshima Kazuo, 1987
65 x 4.5 x 17

Bamboo toy guns became especially popular during the Japanese campaigns in China, from 1935 onward. The barrel made from a hollow bamboo stem could fire small stones. Other bamboo toys included water guns and marionettes.

118.1–30 Whirligigs

(take tombo)
Made by Hiroshima Kazuo, 1987
15 x 1.5 x 19

Japanese children called these toys "bamboo dragonflies." Mr. Hiroshima shaved strips of bamboo into propeller shapes and attached them to sticks at their midpoints; a strong spin between the palms of the hands, right hand leading forward, sets them flying.

Objects Made from Other Materials

119.1–10 Vine hip baskets

(tsuzura tego)
Made by Kōrogi Sakai, 1987
34 x 24 x 30

A vine hip basket was used for collecting *shiitake* in both spring and autumn or for picking tea in the spring. Compared to the bamboo hip baskets used for the same purposes (nos. 59–61), it is lighter and more resilient yet can hold quite large loads; for these reasons, it is more widespread than the bamboo baskets in this area.

Kōrogi Sakai (1908–1989) of Gokase Village once noted that nearly every Hinokage-area village used to have at least one man skilled in vine basketry. The raw material is the wild vine known locally as *tsuzura,* which is collected in the fall and stored in bundles under the eaves of the house or barn. At the beginning of February the vines are laid out on the ground and covered with rice straw for two days, to add flexibility and durability (a vine basket will last fifty years). Mr. Kōrogi used to make one each twelve-hour workday; at that pace, he would exhaust his supply of vines just in time for tea picking in May.

Two thirty-meter-long vines are needed for the horizontal weaving strands. Good vines once grew among maple or beech trees in the forests, but many of the mountainsides have been turned into cultivated—and carefully weeded—groves of cedar and cypress. Vines that have grown around trees cannot be used, since they break at their nodes. One-year-old vines growing along the ground are ideal.

119.1, 119.2

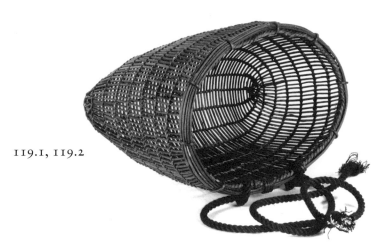

120 "Chinese" backpack frame

(tōjingarui)
Made by Kai Katsuyoshi, 1986
52 × 40 × 122

This type of backpack frame is constructed from two long pieces of wood joined by crosspieces and two shorter pieces of wood projecting at an angle, on which the load would be stacked. Farmers load firewood, brushwood, bales of charcoal, sheaves of rice straw, bundles of grass, and other bulky cargo onto the frame and carry the freight on their backs. Rice-straw shoulder straps and pad protect the bearer's back and shoulders. The term "Chinese" connotes "continental" things in general, and the structure resembles the *chige* used in Korea for similar functions. The basketmaker who constructed this frame was born in 1907 and now lives in Hakamadani hamlet in Hinokage; until 1989, when he had a stroke, he would make *tōjingarui* for neighbors on request. Like the bamboo *karui*, this frame is indispensable for work in the mountains.

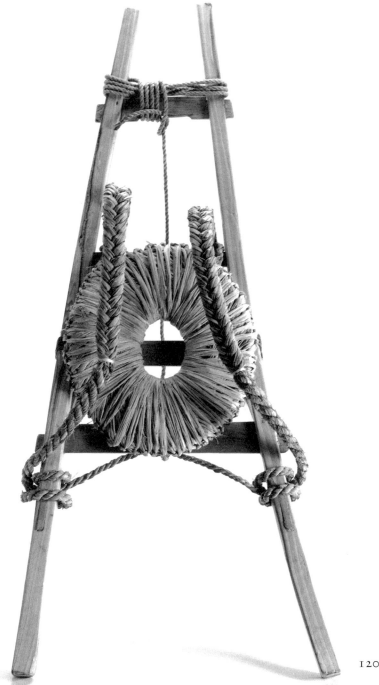

120

121.1–126.1

121.1–10 Backpack basket shoulder straps

(karuinoo)
Made by Hashimoto Fusae, 1987
10 x 5 x 80

Plaited from rice straw by a woman from Kūchi hamlet in Hinokage, these flat straps were attached to *karui* backpack baskets as shoulder straps. Women occasionally made the straps for creels and backpacks.

122.1–10 Rice-straw sandals

(wara zōri)
Made by Hashimoto Fusae, 1987
25 x 11 x 6

The soles of these basic sandals are plaited from rice straw. Twisted straw ropes bound with colorful strips of cotton cloth form the straps. A thin straw rope keeps the sandals paired until they are used.

123.1–5 Half-sole sandals

(ashinaka waraji)
Made by Kawashima Tokumatsu, 1987
20 x 11 x 6

The short soles of these rice-straw sandals would cover only the ball of the wearer's foot. They were made this way so as to counteract slipping when worn in the river. Mr. Kawashima, born in Unama hamlet in 1900, learned how to weave these as a teenager. He opened a clock store in Hinokage, which he closed upon retiring in 1980, and although he is now bedridden, he was skillful at all sorts of handwork and carpentry into his eighties. Aside from weaving straw sandals, he could also make braided straw ornaments and ropes for use in shrine festivals.

124.1–5 Work sandals

(sagyō waraji)
Made by Kawashima Tokumatsu, 1987
25 X 11 X 7

The construction of rice-straw work sandals, which fit tightly to the heel and sole, made them suitable for farming or mountain chores as well as for walking and working.

125.1–5 Travel sandals

(ryōkō waraji)
Made by Kawashima Tokumatsu, 1987
25 X 11 X 9

Made for walking long distances, rice-straw travel sandals were held in place by cords that wrapped around the ankles.

126.1–5 Feudal lord's sandals

(tonosama zōri)
Made by Kawashima Tokumatsu, 1987
26 X 12 X 6.5

From the seventeenth to the mid-nineteenth century, the military lords of the Nobeoka domain are said to have worn rice-straw sandals like these, constructed with double soles to cushion the bottoms of the feet.

127.1–5 Cattle shoes

(ushi no kutsu)
Made by Kawashima Tokumatsu, 1987
19 X 10 X 12

Rice-straw sandals like these were fitted to all four hooves of cattle when they were used as pack animals, to protect their hooves from small stones or other debris that could cause injury.

128.1–5 Horse shoes

(uma no kutsu)
Made by Kawashima Tokumatsu, 1987
17 X 12 X 13

These shoes served the same function for horses as no. 127 did for cattle.

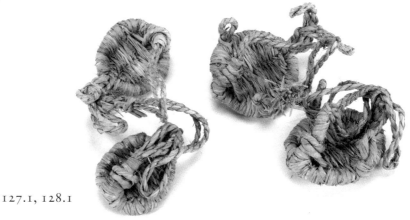

127.1, 128.1

129, 131.1–3

129 Rice coffer

(ohitsu)
Made by Iiboshi Matao, 1986
36.5 x 36.5 x 13

This bentwood container was constructed of silk-tree wood, which was shaved into thin strips, steamed, bent into shape, and fastened with strips of cherry bark. A rice coffer is used for serving cooked rice, especially in winter, and has the advantageous properties of retaining heat and absorbing moisture, so that the rice stays warm but does not become soggy. (It is the winter counterpart of the rice-storage basket used in summer.) Iiboshi Matao was born in 1926 in Takachiho. Raised in a farming family, Mr. Iiboshi later worked in the mines in Fukuoka Prefecture until he could no longer keep up the physical

130

demands of the work. At the age of fifty-one, he taught himself to make *karui, shōke,* and bentwood containers, and he opened his own craft shop in Hinokage. He stopped working in 1987, when he suffered a stroke.

130 Steamer

(seiro)
Made by Iiboshi Matao, 1986
25.5 x 25.5 x 17

This is another bentwood product made from silk-tree wood. Fitted with a bamboo lattice shelf, it could be used for steaming foods over a pot of boiling water.

131.1–3 Lunchboxes

(menpa)
16.5 x 16.5 x 7.5
Made by Iiboshi Matao, 1986

These bentwood objects crafted from silk-tree wood are made to be portable lunchboxes, but the lids and bodies can also serve as a set of bowls. The wood retains heat and absorbs moisture.

132.1–6 Miniature floor mats

(kogata tatami)
Made by Satō Riichi, 1987
60.5 x 60.5 x 6

Satō Riichi, a professional tatami maker in Hinokage, made six small versions of a tatami mat for displaying the baskets. The thick rice-straw foundation is covered with a mat woven of fragrant grass and edged with fabric.

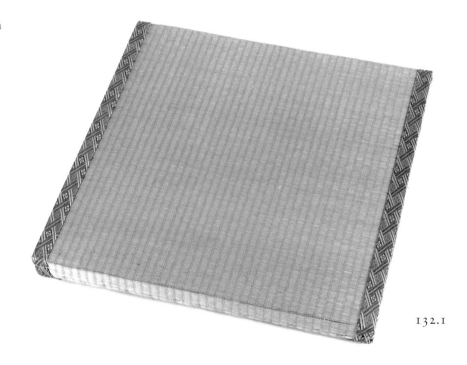

132.1

Raw Materials and Tools

EXACTING SELECTION of raw materials and adroit use of specialized tools distinguish the work of the professional basketmaker from that of the amateur. Whenever possible, Mr. Hiroshima cuts his bamboo in late autumn, when the stalks are least vulnerable to insect infestation. He may find no more than a few suitable stalks on a hillside full of bamboo—and large bamboo stands are rapidly disappearing as slopes are cleared for other commercial trees.

Mr. Hiroshima began assembling his collection of tools while he was still an apprentice, and he has maintained long-term relationships with the blacksmiths and foundry that supply tools of good quality. When he is seated in his workshop making a basket, all his tools are within reach in his wooden toolbox or hanging on the wall at his back.

133 Sample of *hachiku* bamboo

(Phyllostachys nigra, var. *henonis)*
13 X 10 X 257

This and the following bamboo samples represent the types of bamboo that grow in the Hinokage area. *Hachiku* bamboo can be used for nearly everything a basketmaker produces.

134.1–2 Samples of *kurotake* bamboo

(Phyllostachys bambusoides)
28 X 17 X 262

Kurotake is another all-purpose bamboo. It is known more generally as *madake*. Compared to *hachiku*, *kurotake* nodes are somewhat closer together and the mature stalks are larger in diameter.

135 Sample of *chinchikudake* bamboo

6 X 4 X 255

This thin, springy bamboo is a member of the *Sasa* species (its standard name is *hōraichiku*). Since it bends easily, Mr. Hiroshima uses it for finishing the rims of stoppers for eel traps or creels or for binding other small openings.

134, 133, 135

136 Sample of *tsuzura* vine

95 X 37 X 10

Tsuzura vine, like this sample from Gokase Village, is used for securing handles, binding the mouths of winnows, and as the raw material for vine hip baskets (no. 119).

136

137 Bamboo-splitting knife

(takewari hōchō)
Made by Kai Teruyoshi, 1987
37.5 X 4 X 3

In 1931, Mr. Hiroshima commissioned a set of bamboo-working tools from Sasahara Chōhei of Miyaji hamlet, Ichinomiya Town, Kumamoto Prefecture, after learning that he had made tools for the gifted basketmaker, Ushi-don. Mr. Sasahara's workshop went out of business in 1955, and five years later Mr. Hiroshima employed Kai Teruyoshi, a Hinokage blacksmith, who continued to make Mr. Hiroshima's tools until 1991. These forged steel tools (nos. 137–43) made for the Nakamura Collection were based on the original set made by Mr. Sasahara.

This style of knife is used for all basic hand processes relating to basketmaking—splitting the bamboo lengths, shaping the weaving strips *(higo),* and cutting them.

138 Tool for binding rims

(hira fuchimaki)
Made by Kai Teruyoshi, 1987
17 X 2.5 X 3

Mr. Hiroshima uses wide strips of bamboo for binding the rims of many basket forms in his repertory. With this kind of blade he pushes the strip firmly into place as he wraps. He uses a tool like this in conjunction with an awl (no. 139).

139 Awl for binding rims

(mizo fuchimaki)
Made by Kai Teruyoshi, 1987
20 X 3 X 3.8

Mr. Hiroshima uses an awl like this to open spaces in the rim of a basket, then he winds a flat strip of bamboo through the holes around the rim to make a smooth finished edge.

140 Faceting knife

(mentori hōchō)
Made by Kai Teruyoshi, 1987
30.6 X 5 X 3

With a faceting knife, Mr. Hiroshima smooths and rounds the weaving strips *(higo)* for baskets such as storage baskets for cooked rice (nos. 1, 27, and 28) or rice-rinsing colanders (nos. 41–42). Rounded strips create a smooth surface to which rice grains will not cling.

141 Die for weaving strips

(busoroe)
Made by Kai Teruyoshi and Kai Sanji, 1987
18 x 19 x 5.5

A blacksmith and a carpenter collaborated to make this version of the tool that Mr. Hiroshima learned about in 1939 from a basketmaker from Kagoshima Prefecture. The distance between the angled blades can be adjusted according to the width of weaving strips *(higo)* required; drawing the strips between the blades assures a uniform size.

142 Trimming blade

(ishizuri)
Made by Kai Teruyoshi, 1987
19 x 8 x 4

A trimming blade is used to prepare the bamboo strips that will be bent and inserted into the woven basket as reinforcers or strengtheners *(chikaradake)*. The sharp, angled blade shaves off the flesh on the insides of the strips at the points where they are to be bent, so as to make them easier to manipulate and keep them from breaking.

143 Awl for binding edges with vines

(kazura tōshi)
Made by Kai Teruyoshi, 1987
15.5 x 5.5 x 25

This type of awl is used specifically in making winnows for grains and beans (not represented in this catalogue). When the basket edge is finished by attaching a wide strip of bamboo with lengths of vine (no. 136), this tool opens the holes through which the vine is passed. Mr. Hiroshima purchased an awl like this from the widow of Sasaki Hajime, who specialized in winnows.

144 Bow-shaped saw

(yumi noko)
Purchased from Usui Foundry, Osaka; gift of Hiroshima Kazuo
51.7 x 12.2 x 2

This thin, sharp blade leaves clean edges when cutting bamboo stalks into required lengths before making any bamboo vessel. Mr. Hiroshima has been ordering these saws from the same foundry since 1932.

145 Pliers

(penchi)
Purchased from Takahashi Hardware Store
16 x 5 x 1.5
Mr. Hiroshima uses pliers for various processes, including cutting lengths of wire to attach rims to trays (no. 34).

146 Gimlet

(kiri)
Purchased from Takahashi Hardware Store
25.8 x 1.6 x 1.6

With a fine-pointed tool like this, Mr. Hiroshima can punch small holes in the rim of a basket and through these holes pass the pegs used to secure the handle (no. 27).

147 Stake-cutting blade

(kuikiri)
Purchased from Takahashi Hardware Store
12 x 4.5 x 1.2

A blade like this is needed to cut off the ends of the weaving strips *(higo)* in places where a bamboo-splitting knife (no. 137) or even a small knife (no. 148) cannot fit.

148 Small knife

(kogatana)
Purchased from Takahashi Hardware Store
25.5 x 3.4 x 17

A small knife is used for delicate cutting work on small objects such as stoppers for eel traps (nos. 24–26), where a bamboo-splitting knife (no. 137) would be difficult to use.

137–153, 173

149 Hatchet

(nata)
Purchased from a hardware store in
Nobeoka; gift of Hiroshima Kazuo
60 x 14 x 2.8

Mr. Hiroshima uses a hatchet to cut
bamboo in the grove and then to cut
lengths of bamboo to the required size
for specific projects. This hatchet was
made by a blacksmith specializing in
farming tools.

150 Folding ruler

(orijaku)
Purchased from Takahashi Hardware
Store
20 x 1.5 x 1.4

Mr. Hiroshima uses a folding ruler
like this, which is marked with metric
lengths, not only for convenience but
also to fill orders placed with metric
measure. Mr. Hiroshima learned to
make baskets based on the *shaku-sun-
bu* measurement system, which is documented on a standard "yardstick"
type of ruler *(kujirajaku)* used by carpenters and others.

151 Toolbox

(takezaiku dōgu bako)
Made by Kai Sanji, 1987
48.7 x 27 x 23.7

This wooden toolbox is a replica of
the box that Mr. Hiroshima had
made in 1941 and still uses. He paid
the carpenter who built the original 5
yen; this replica by Kai Sanji of Yato
cost 8,000 yen. Mr. Hiroshima used
to place all his tools in a backpack
basket *(karui)* and carry them from
house to house, where he filled orders
for baskets. He had the box made
when he stopped his itinerant work.

152 Auxiliary tool for bamboo work

(takezaiku hojogu)
Made by Kai Sanji, 1987
9 x 9 x 26

Conical stoppers for eel traps (nos.
24–26) are woven around wooden
tools like this and no. 153.

153 Auxiliary tool for bamboo work

(takezaiku hojogu)
Made by Kai Sanji, 1987
6.4 x 6.4 x 25

Narrower version of no. 152.

154.1–2 Auxiliary tools for bamboo work

(takezaiku hojogu)
Made at Koda Woodworking
Factory, 1987
70 x 64 x 6.5

To weave *shiitake* sieves with precise sizes of mesh (nos. 62–65), Mr. Hiroshima relies on the template engraved on his work table (no. 156). As he weaves, he holds the bamboo strips in place between two identical wooden pieces like these, which were made at a factory in Hinokage. He keeps the wooden pieces in place until he adds the rim to the sieve.

155 Round work table

(marugata takezaiku seisakudai)
Made by Kai Sanji, 1987
37.5 x 37.5 x 27.5

Mr. Hiroshima uses a work table like this when he weaves the "chrysanthe-mum"-shaped center, with radiating elements, of baskets such as the bean-paste sieve (no. 51) or the tray for drying *shiitake* (no. 80).

156 Square work table

(kakugata takezaiku seisakudai)
Made by Kai Sanji, 1987
82 x 82 x 5

Mr. Hiroshima uses a square work table like this, which is engraved with a geometric pattern, to help him weave a uniform mesh for his *shiitake* sieves (nos. 62–65).

154.1–2, 155, 156

Substitutes for Bamboo Baskets

THE DECLINE in bamboo basketmaking is related to the emergence of plastic and vinyl products, which first appeared in the mid-fifties. The strongest impact was felt by wooden bucket makers. Wooden buckets and barrels once widely used for water, pickles, and other purposes gave way completely to plastic replacements. Bamboo baskets nearly suffered the same fate. In a flash, plastic vessels replicating most bamboo shapes appeared in every household; however, certain bamboo items that either could not be replaced by mass-produced substitutes or were not in enough demand to be manufactured have continued to be essential in regional niches.

Plastic baskets are made efficiently and uniformly by machine; they come in colors such as red, blue, yellow, and green; and they cost much less than custom-made bamboo baskets. Because they are so inexpensive, they do not have to be used with the same care as bamboo implements. Their disposability is part of their fascination. However, plastic baskets do not have some of the appeal of baskets made from natural materials; since they are not woven like bamboo they do not drain as well; they melt when exposed to flame; when cold they become brittle and easily break. Despite these drawbacks, they came into use everywhere. Beginning in the kitchen where they replaced the bamboo colander, plastic substitutes supplanted transporting baskets, baskets for storing live fish, and other vessels required in large quantities. Metal mesh substitutes also became widespread.

Naturally the number of bamboo craftsmen decreased. When they realized that even if they made baskets they couldn't sell them, most basketmakers who were able changed their occupations. The number of young people willing to spend three or four years virtually without salary in order to learn the bamboo craftsman's skills drastically declined, and the surviving bamboo craftsmen are now mostly elderly.

Some substitutes for bamboo baskets are handmade from different materials; others are commercially produced with the backing of cooperatives. In the early seventies, the head of the Hinokage Agricultural Cooperative used Mr. Hiroshima's *shiitake* sieves (nos. 62–65) as models for commissioning plastic versions. They were quickly adopted by *shiitake* processors and helped increase profits.

157 Plastic basket for holding live eels

(ikashi kago)
Purchased from Kōno Bait and Tackle Store
66 x 66 x 37
Fishermen's cooperatives in Nobeoka and elsewhere throughout Japan distribute this sort of plastic container for fish.

158 Plastic basket for holding live eels

(ikashi kago)
Purchased from Kōno Bait and Tackle Store
45 x 45 x 28.5
Smaller version of no. 157.

159 Galvanized steel canteen for bait fish

(otorigan)
Made by Kai Tokio, 1970; gift of Hidaka Kinmatsu
28 x 28 x 14.5
This handmade vessel of bent steel and plaited wire was made for holding sweetfish, which are used as bait *(otori)* to catch other sweetfish (compare no. 114).

157–161

160 Vinyl trap for fish

(hibi)
Purchased from Hiroshima Store
15 x 15 x 28
This fish trap made of transparent vinyl (compare nos. 19–22) would have been used to capture fish lured by the smell of worms inside the trap.

161 Wire mesh trap for river crabs

(hibi)
Purchased from Hiroshima Store
67 x 46 x 3.5
Both openings of this trap (compare nos. 20–21) would be baited with fragrant fish or chicken bones to attract river crabs.

162 Wire mesh storage basket

(shokuhin kago)
Purchased from Hirakawa Hardware Store
40 x 30 x 16
Like the bamboo storage basket for dried fish (nos. 29–31), this covered mesh container is suspended from the ceiling for safe storage of food products. The metal version became widespread from the mid-fifties onward.

163 Wire mesh storage basket

(shokuhin kago)
Purchased from Hirakawa Hardware Store
35 x 35 x 23
Round version of no. 162.

164 Stainless steel mesh colander

(zaru)
Purchased from Takahashi Hardware Store
46.5 x 40.5 x 14.5

This stainless steel version of a bamboo colander (nos. 35–39 and 41–45) was used for washing and draining rice, grains, vegetables, and other foodstuffs.

165.1–5 Set of plastic *shiitake* sieves

(naba tōshi)
Purchased from Hinokage Agricultural Cooperative
77 x 77 x 10.5

Shiitake farmers and commercial growers used plastic sieves with standardized mesh widths to grade sizes of dried *shiitake* for commercial sales (compare nos. 62–65).

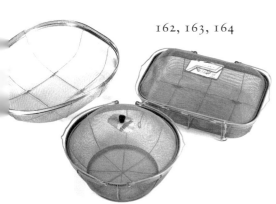

162, 163, 164

166 Rectangular plastic container

Purchased from Hinokage Agricultural Cooperative
52 x 36.5 x 30.3

Based on the shape of the bicycle basket (nos. 72–74), standard-sized, stackable containers like this are used to sort and transport farm products.

167 Plastic backpack basket

Purchased from Hinokage Agricultural Cooperative
52 x 40.8 x 49.5

This backpack basket for harvesting and transporting agricultural produce is marketed by the Agricultural Cooperative Union.

168.1–2 Plastic stone-carrying fan

(ishi mi)
Purchased from Hinokage Agricultural Cooperative
42 x 40 x 14

A plastic substitute for carrying fans (nos. 88–89), this type of basket is used for moving stones or clods of earth.

169 Plastic fertilizer basket

(koe ire)
Purchased from Hinokage Agricultural Cooperative
40.5 x 30 x 17

As a plastic replacement for a bamboo fertilizer basket (no. 40), this type of basket is used for transporting various types of manure and compost.

Additional Baskets and Tools

MR. HIROSHIMA provided these sieves and tools for the collection in July 1989.

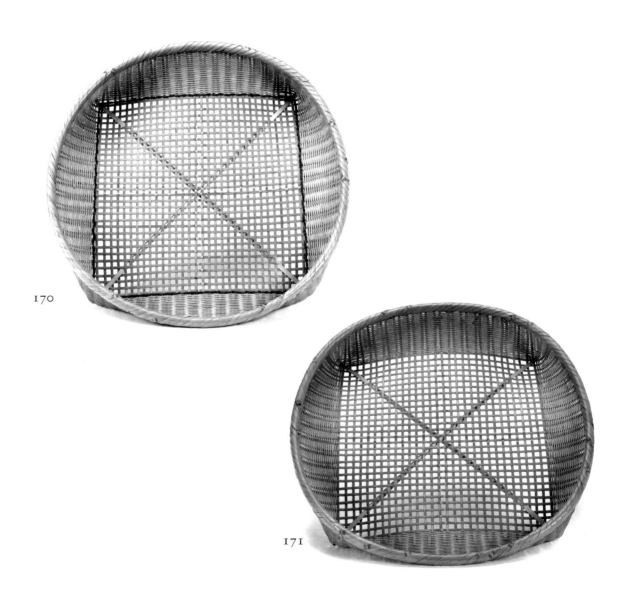

170

171

170 Chaff sieve

(momi tōshi), 2-*bu* mesh
Made by Hiroshima Kazuo, ca. 1989
56 x 56 x 12.5

A smaller version of no. 46, this type of sieve allowed rice grains *(momi)* to pass through, leaving husks and debris behind. It was also a good size for cleaning other grains and beans (such as wheat, barley, millet, *azuki* beans, or soybeans) of their husks or dried pods.

171 Chaff sieve

(momi tōshi), 2.5-*bu* mesh
Made by Hiroshima Kazuo, ca. 1989
56 x 56 x 12.5

Smaller version of no. 47.

172 Bamboo-splitting tool

(jū monji)
Made by Hiroshima Kazuo, ca. 1989
15 x 15 x 4

Shaped like the Chinese character for the numeral "ten," from which it derives its Japanese name, this wooden tool would be used in the first step of preparing bamboo for basketmaking, when the stalk is split lengthwise into quarters.

173 Clippers

(senteibasami)
Purchased from Takahashi Hardware Store
18 x 5 x 2

With clippers like these (see photograph on page 138), Mr. Hiroshima cut the excess length off of weaving strips *(higo)* after he had completed the weaving process and before he had bound the rim.

174 Hammer

(kanazuchi)
Purchased from Takahashi Hardware Store
33 x 11.5 x 2.1

Mr. Hiroshima used this type of hammer to drive bamboo pegs or to secure the ends of weaving strips within the woven structure.

174, 172

The Annual Work Cycle of a Hinokage Farming Family

Nakamura Nori

Mʏ ʜᴏᴍᴇ is in the Hinokage hamlet of Miyamizu, formerly the administrative center of Nanaori Village. Nakamura Kenji is my nephew. In the past, successive male heads of the Nakamura family served as village headman, a position equivalent to mayor before 1868. For some three hundred years, my family was a prominent landowner in Miyamizu, involved in sake brewing and forestry. Following the redistribution of land after World War II, they stopped leasing land to tenants and undertook rice farming themselves.

I was born in 1929 as the third daughter in a family of seven children. My husband's family's spacious old farmhouse with its outbuildings stands at the top of a long stone staircase and was once the center for many community activities. My husband and I continue to work on our farm, where we keep two cows, one calf, five chickens, and a dog. Our youngest son, who works in the Hinokage town office, assists us on weekends during the busy seasons of May–June and October–November; we have two other sons, who have married and moved away from the area. Our work cycle has followed the routines I describe for the last fifty years.

January

- Make fermented soybean paste (miso), using soybeans, rice yeast, and salt. The rice yeast is homemade from purchased starter and broken rice grains (not suitable for sale) husked at home.
- Prepare dried cakes called *kakimochi*. Water drawn at the coldest time of the year (late January–early February) is used to cook glutinous rice *(mochigome)* together with a small amount of sugar; the cooked, sweetened rice is pounded (in a mortar with a wooden mallet) into a paste, thinly sliced, and dried. When served as a winter snack, it is deep-fried and becomes crisp and puffy.
- Cut firewood to last the year. Firewood is required for kitchen stoves and heating the bath.
- Trim sections of wood for use in growing *shiitake* mushrooms. Trees felled the previous November are cut into 1.2-meter lengths.

February

- Continue cutting year's supply of firewood.
- Inject *shiitake* spores in the tree lengths. Harvest *shiitake* from tree lengths injected twenty months earlier.
- Fertilize and prune tea bushes.
- Plow rice paddies.
- Plant Irish potatoes and spinach.

March

- Harvest *shiitake.*
- Plant groves of trees, including cedar, cypress, and trees for raising *shiitake.*
- Sell calves (approximately eight months after birth).
- Prepare fertilizer from manure collected in cow barn; fertilize and till rice paddies.
- Plant seeds for spring vegetables. Plant sweet potatoes in covered seedbed (heated with manure). Plant taro in field. Plant ginger.
- Plant seeds for beefsteak plant (also known as *akashiso,* or red perilla) for use in making salt-preserved plums *(umeboshi).*
- Harvest cabbage.

April

- Till rice paddies.
- Clean debris from channels that carry water to paddies. (The channels carry water from upriver for all the paddies in the community; in November each household pays an annual fee, based on square footage of paddies, toward repairing and maintaining the channels.)
- Harvest meadow grass.
- Sterilize soil for use in rice seedling bed.
- Dig bamboo shoots.
- Harvest wild greens; April is the most abundant season for wild greens, including *warabi, udo, zenmai,* and *dara.*

May

- Harvest tea.
- Sow rice seed in hothouse seedbed. About three weeks later, use planting machine to begin transplanting seedlings to paddies.
- Regulate water level in paddies.
- Plant kitchen garden, including tomatoes, cucumbers, eggplant, soybeans for eating green, melons for pickling, and pumpkin.

June

- Continue transplanting rice seedlings (to mid-month). Regulate water level in paddies and cut weeds along edges.
- Transplant sweet potatoes to field. Weed taro. Plant corn.
- Harvest Irish potatoes, plums, peaches, loquats, peas, and broad beans.

July

- In the forest, weed groves of seedlings planted in March.
- Weed and manage water level in paddies.
- Weed dry fields.
- By mid-month, plant soybeans (for making fermented soybean paste) and *azuki* beans (for use in steamed-bun filling and cooked with glutinous rice for festivals and celebrations).

August

- Regulate water level in paddies and cut weeds along edges.
- Weed groves of seedlings.
- Harvest produce in kitchen garden.
- Pick beefsteak plant and make salt-preserved plums. From remaining plants prepare pickled beefsteak leaves (layer with salt for one month, wrap in *kombu* seaweed, embed in fermented bean paste for six months).

September

- Cut and dry meadow grass.
- Harvest autumn vegetables, chestnuts, and persimmons.
- Plant early season Chinese cabbage, spinach, edible chrysanthemum, and lettuce varieties.

October

- Harvest rice. Dry rice straw (together with meadow grass, rice straw is used for feeding cattle from January through April).
- Harvest corn, sweet potatoes, and taro.
- Pick *kabosu* citrus and make vinegar (used in citrus-and-soy sauce dip for dishes like winter stews and simmered bean curd).
- Transplant giant radish *(daikon)* along with late-season Chinese cabbage.

November

- Cut trees for use in raising *shiitake*. Harvest *shiitake*.
- Harvest soybeans, *azuki* beans, and other small beans. Harvest devil's tongue *(konnyaku)*, carrots, burdock root, and spinach.
- Send unhusked rice to agricultural cooperative to be sold.
- Pick citron *(yuzu)* and prepare *yuzu* products. Pick and process kumquat.
- Plant peas, onions, cabbage, and pickling greens. Plant meadow grass (Italian and clover).
- Prepare varieties of giant radish pickles (such as *takuan*). Make pickles from ginger, carrots, giant radish, and Chinese cabbage.

December

- Spread out posts for use in raising *shiitake*.
- Prepare dried shredded giant radish *(kiriboshi daikon)* and dried persimmons.
- Preserve giant radish, Chinese cabbage, and ginger.
- Toward the end of the month, prepare for New Year's celebrations: steam glutinous rice, pound in mortar, and make rice cakes *(mochi)*; make homemade wheat noodles *(udon)*, pickles, devil's tongue jelly, and other items. Send gifts of *shiitake, mochi,* and rice to relatives and friends living far away.

Growing Rice

- At the end of April, begin sowing seedling rice in seedbed. Make two or three more plantings between the first of May and mid-month. Spacing out the planting allows for all the transplanting to be done by three household members. The seedlings can be transplanted into the flooded and prepared paddies twenty to twenty-five days after sowing seeds. The seedlings must be weeded within ten days after transplanting.
- From mid-July, when seedlings are well rooted and growing, begin reducing amount of water in paddies over a period of seven to ten days. The last week of July, flood the paddies again.
- Early September, when rice heads begin filling out, broadcast pesticide to prevent blight and insect infestations.
- The third week in September, ten days before beginning harvest, reduce water level in paddies. Begin harvest about 3 October. Dry threshed rice 24 hours in mechanical dryer to bring moisture level down to 15 percent; preserve as unhusked rice for government purchase in November.
- From December until March, spread fertilizer in the paddies and plow. Mid-April, ten days before transplanting seedlings, flood paddies with water, reinforce bunds between paddies, and plow once again.

Raising Shiitake

- In mid-November, cut trees for logs to be used in raising *shiitake*. Starting first half of January, cut to 1.2-meter lengths.
- February through March, inject mushroom spores in logs, store in locale facing southeast, protected from sunlight and strong winds.
- Approximately twenty months after injecting, begin harvesting *shiitake*. Autumn harvest occurs from September to October; spring harvest occurs from December to end of April. The logs will continue bearing mushrooms for about five years.

Bibliography

This bibliography emphasizes publications devoted to utilitarian rather than art baskets, with ethnographic background regarding the production, distribution, and use of such baskets. It also tries to cover the limited material available in English.

"Amiagerareta yō to bi: Hyūga no takezaiku wo tazunete" (Woven use and beauty: Visiting the bamboo crafts of Hyūga Province). *Ginka* 24 (winter 1975): 127–34. Evocative essay on baskets of three regions of the former Hyūga Province (now Miyazaki Prefecture), including Takachiho.

Austin, Robert, and Koichiro Ueda. Photographs by Dana Levy. *Bamboo*. New York and Tokyo: Weatherhill, 1970. A sweeping view of the myriad uses of bamboo in Japan and elsewhere in Asia, with a section on bamboo cultivation.

Farrelly, David. *The Book of Bamboo*. San Francisco: Sierra Club Books, 1984. Exhaustive study of bamboo from a worldwide perspective.

Hasebe Mitsuhiko et al., eds. *Modern Bamboo Craft*. Tokyo: Crafts Gallery, National Museum of Modern Art, 1985. The first postwar Japanese exhibition to treat bamboo craft exhaustively, focusing on art baskets and industrial design. Two essays, in English, on historical and contemporary bamboo craft.

Hauge, Victor, and Takako Hauge. *Folk Traditions in Japanese Art*. Washington, D.C.: International Exhibitions Foundation, 1978. Exhibition catalogue that includes a range of regional utilitarian baskets.

"Hiroshima Kazuo-san to Ōshima Shinko Kyōkai" (Hiroshima Kazuo and the Ōshima Development Association). *Nihon no mingei* 318 (March 1982): 14. Discusses Mr. Hiroshima's first-prize award in 1981 at the twenty-third annual folk craft exhibition in Osaka and the UMK Miyazaki Television profile of him, "Take ni ikiru" (Heart of Japan: Living through Bamboo).

Holme, Charles. "The Uses of Bamboo in Japan," in *Japanese Crafts: Materials and Their Applications*. Edited by B. Hickman. London: Fine Books Oriental, 1977. Reprint of an essay from the Transactions and Proceedings of the

Japan Society, London, which gives a sense of baskets in common urban use circa 1892–1915.

Inagaki Naotomo. "Kagozukuri nyūmon ki" (Record of a basketmaking apprenticeship). *Aruku-miru-kiku* 131 (January 1978): 4–31. A young Japanese man records his three months' apprenticeship to a basketmaker in Kumamoto Prefecture, west of Hinokage.

Kudō Kazuyoshi. "Takezaiku wo tazuneru 1" (In search of bamboo crafts 1). *Aruku-miru-kiku* 75 (May 1973): 4–41. An ethnographer discusses regional basket production in northern, northeastern, and southern Japan.

———. "Takezaiku wo tazuneru 2" (In search of bamboo crafts 2). *Aruku-miru-kiku* 94 (December 1974): 4–31. Further investigation of regional basketmaking in northeastern, eastern, and far southern Japan and in Taiwan, followed by summaries of major basketmaking centers and distribution routes throughout Japan.

———. "Zaruya hōmonki" (Visit to a *zaru* maker). *Aruku-miru-kiku* 131 (January 1978): 32–35. A profile of a basketmaker in Saitama Prefecture, near Tokyo, who specializes in multipurpose hemispherical baskets called *zaru*, equivalent to Hinokage *shōke* colanders.

———. *Japanese Bamboo Baskets.* Tokyo, New York, and San Francisco: Kodansha International, in collaboration with the Japan Research Institute for Tourism and Cultural Resources, 1980. Discussion of Japanese utilitarian baskets (richly illustrated with black-and-white photographs) in terms of form, function, materials, and regional characteristics.

———. *Kurashi no naka no take to wara* (Bamboo and straw in everyday life). Tokyo: Gyōsei, 1982. The most exhaustive book in Japanese on techniques, regional styles, distribution, and usage of utilitarian baskets in Japan (including Okinawa), with comparisons to Taiwan. Many of the baskets also appear in *Japanese Bamboo Baskets* by the same author.

Massy, Patricia. *Sketches of Japanese Crafts and the People Who Make Them.* Tokyo: Japan Times, 1980. Includes an introduction to basket forms from Kagoshima, centering on varieties of flat trays *(bara)* used there like the *shōke* in Hinokage.

McCallum, Toshiko M. *Containing Beauty: Japanese Bamboo Flower Baskets.* Los Angeles: UCLA Museum of Cultural History, 1988. Overview of baskets made to display flower arrangements. Includes detailed discussion of production processes and terminology of the art basket.

McClure, F. A. *The Bamboos.* Washington, D.C.: Smithsonian Institution Press, 1994. Reissue of a 1966 study by a pioneering American horticulturist who studied Chinese bamboo and advocated the plant's propagation and wider use in North America.

Misumi Kan. *Sanka shakai no kenkyū* (Research on the social structure of migratory groups). Vol. 35, *Misumi Kan zenshū* (Collected works of Misumi Kan). Tokyo: Bōnenji Shuppan, 1965. Study of the migratory mountain-dwelling people known as *sanka*, who made their living until the fifties by selling baskets and other bamboo products.

Mizuo Hiroshi. *Takeami* (Bamboo constructions). Vol. 2, *Nihon no zōkei* (Japanese forms). Kyoto: Tankōsha, 1970. Analysis of diverse bamboo objects according to categories of weave, illustrated by serial photographs of basketmakers at work and regional basket types.

Nippon Mingu Gakkai, ed. *Take to mingu* (Bamboo and popular crafts). Vol. 5, *Nippon Mingu Gakkai ronshū* (Memoirs of the Society for the Material Cultures of Japan). Tokyo: Yūzankaku, 1991. Eight essays by folklorists and ethnographers on aspects of utilitarian bamboo crafts.

Okiura Kazuteru. *Take no min-zokushi* (Folklore of bamboo). Iwanami shinshō (Iwanami new issues). No. 187. Tokyo: Iwanami Shoten, 1991. Historic view of the meanings and uses of bamboo in Japanese culture and the social status of bamboo craftsmen.

Saint-Gilles, Amaury. *Mingei: Japan's Enduring Folk Arts*. Union City, Calif.: Heian International, 1983. Catalogue of regional crafts that includes the salt-draining basket, the winnowing basket, and the bamboo "dragonfly" toy.

Shiono Yonematsu. "Kawa no seikatsushi" (History of life on the river). *Headwater* 4 (1988): 132–38. Part of a special feature on the Hinokage River in a periodical devoted to fishing. Includes presentation of Mr. Hiroshima and his baskets related to fishing, also vine baskets by Kōrogi Sakai and bentwood buckets by Iiboshi Matao.

Tabuchi Satoru, photographer. "Hyūga no takezaiku" (Bamboo crafts of Hyūga Province). *Ginka* 24 (winter 1975): 111–26. Black-and-white photographic study of baskets used in rural Miyazaki Prefecture.

———. "Nihonjin no dōgu—kago" (Baskets: Tools of the Japanese peo-ple). *Ginka* 28 (winter 1976): 5–24. Color photographs presenting baskets in use in several regions of Japan.

Takama Shinji. *The World of Bamboo*. San Francisco: Heian International, 1983. Japan's foremost photographer of bamboo captures in color the forms and patterns of living bamboo and shows uses in Japanese religious rituals, architecture, and crafts.

Waga machi no meikō (Outstanding artisans of our community). Miyazaki: Miyazaki-ken Ginōshi-kai Rengōkai, 1993. Listing of Miyazaki Prefecture craftspeople, including Hiroshima Kazuo, recognized by national and prefectural designation.

Yamada Kumeo. "Yama to umi to machi ni kago wo tazuneru" (Visiting baskets in the mountains, sea, and town). *Ginka* 28 (winter 1976): 25–32. Lyrical essay about uses of baskets by villagers and city dwellers in several regions of Japan.

Index